# KNOTS
## for the Cut

# KNOTS
## for the Cut

### by Ben Selfe

Illustrations by Helen Gee

Quicksilver Publications

First published in the United Kingdom in 2008 by
Quicksilver Publications – quicksilver7@btinternet.com

Cover photograph of Tunnel Tug No. 4, *Gloucester* used by kind permission of the owner, Dr Chris Poole. http://www.cdpoole.co.uk

Back cover photograph of Ben Selfe by TammyLynn Photography www.tammylynn.co.uk.
Unless otherwise stated, photographs by Ben Selfe.

Bristol Rope & Twine Co. www.bristolrope.com

ISBN 978-0-9557600-2-0

Typeset in 14pt Times
Illustrations by Helen Gee of Geewhiz Designs – 07756 914 430
Origination by Patricia J Mills – quicksilver7@btinternet.com
Printed in England by J.H. Haynes & Co. Ltd, Sparkford, Somerset.

# Contents

*Foreword by Clive Field*       *vii*

*Acknowledgements*       *ix*

*Glossary of Terms*       *xi*

*Introduction*       *xiii*

*Chapter 1*   **Rope Maintenance**       1

*Chapter 2*   **Mooring your Boat**       7
     Cow Hitching       8
     Anchor Hitch or Fisherman's Bend       9
     Lighterman's Hitch       10
     Belaying on a T-bar or Cleat       12
     Cheesing Down       14
     Bowlines and Moorings       15
     Crowded Moorings       16
     Correct Mooring Procedures       17
     Bowline on the Bight       17
     Round Turn and Two Half Hitches       20
     Clove Hitch       21

*Chapter 3*   **Joining Rope Together**       22
     Fisherman's Knot       22
     Sheet Bend       23

*Chapter 4*   **Splicing and Whipping**       25
     Eye Splice       25
     Back Splice       28
     Forming a Crown       28
     Straight Splice       32
     Simple Whipping       35

*Chapter 5*   **Turks Heads for Tillers and Tables**       37
     Four Three Turk's Head       38
     Five Three Turk's Head       42
     Five Four Turk's Head       46
     The Ocean Plait Mat       50

*. . . continued overleaf*

*Chapter 6* **Making Your Own Fenders** 55

Tools you will need for fender making 56

Knots you will need to know for fender making 57

Grocer's Hitch 58

Constrictor Knot 59

Making a Bottle Fender 61

Standard finish 66

Footrope finish 67

Wall Knot 68

Attaching your fenders to the vessel 70

*Chapter 7* **Covered Fenders** 71

Cores for Buttons for the Stern 72

Cores for Soft Buttons for the Bow 75

Covering a Button 76

Cores and Covers for Barge Fenders and Tipcats 80

Cores for Dwarf's Trousers 83

Covering Dwarf's Trousers 90

U Fender – Core and Covering 93

*Chapter 8* **Fancy Ropework** 96

Rope Safety Ladder 97

Lanyard Knot 98

Matthew Walker Knot 101

The Legend of the Matthew Walker Knot 104

Donut Fenders 105

Tingle Button 107

Spider Weave 108

Basket Weave 108

Cabin Strings 109

French Senate 116

Doubled French Senate 117

Keyrings and Tiller Tassels 118

The 6-strand Matthew Walker Knot 118

Star Knot 120

Making a Keyring 124

English Senate 124

Tiller Tassels 126

**Ben's Bights 'n Pieces** 127

# Foreword

Anyone who spends any time on a boat anywhere on the UK waterways will inevitably need to know something about ropes, knots and hitches.

Those ropes, knots and hitches connect today's boat user to a past when working boaters relied upon their own skills and ingenuity to ensure the safety and security of their vessel and its valuable cargo.

Boats built for today's leisure market carry today's equivalent of a valuable cargo in their costly fittings: on-board sound systems, computer suites, flat-screen monitors and marble-topped kitchen units.

However, regardless of the value, style, type or age of boat, today's proud skipper must still rely on centuries-old roping techniques to ensure the safety of boat and precious contents. It will need to be manoeuvred with care, slowed to avoid impact, moored securely to bank, bollard or pontoon, or even towed home in the event of breakdown.

*Knots for the Cut* will help us to understand the importance of selecting the correct rope for the job as well as the care, use and stowage of what can literally be a life-line. Further study, practice and creativity will allow us to enhance a boat with decorative ropework invariably born of practical purpose.

Ben Selfe's presence at Saul Junction has added even more interest to this wonderful waterside corner of Gloucestershire. He willingly shares his passion and expertise with anyone with time to stand, watch and listen.

*Knots for the Cut* is a further expression of Ben's generous personality. I recommend you invest some of your own time to study, practice and enjoy the acquisition of at least some of the master's proficiency with ropes, knots and hitches.

*Clive E.R. Field*
*Cotswold Canals Trust*

# Acknowledgements

I would like to thank the International Guild of Knot Tyers for their inspiration and encouragement and the Guild members who freely give their time to teach the different and simpler methods of tying knots. Special thanks to Ken Nelson who originally taught me the method for tying cabin strings many years ago.

Grateful thanks are due to my editor, publisher and partner, Trish Mills. Without her publishing skills and expertise, patience and perseverance, this book would never have materialised.

Sincere thanks to Helen Gee for her enthusiasm and quick thinking in interpreting my demonstrations into her unique and wonderful illustrations.

Thanks also go to Pete and Chrissie Ballinger, for being guinea pigs and testing some of the instructions in order to make sure I said what I meant to say.

Also my thanks to the Bristol Rope & Twine Company who have faithfully kept me supplied with a variety of ropes, cord and twine over the years. Acknowledgements to C. Ruth.

I hope this book will be useful to you. I have done my best to be clear and concise. If you have any comments or constructive criticisms, please feel free to contact me.

*Ben Selfe*
*Knot Krazy*

# Glossary of Terms and Abbreviations

Some of the terms used in this book may be unfamiliar, so here is a clarification of the ones that might cause some head scratching.

| | |
|---|---|
| Bight | A loop formed in a rope |
| Fall | The part of the rope not currently in use |
| Hank | Coil of rope lashed and ready to hang |
| Lock off | Trapping or securing the working end under another strand. |
| Thumb knot | Simple overhand knot, e.g. first part of tying shoelaces |
| Tuck | A strand of rope passed through a loop and snugged up |
| Working end | End of rope currently in use |

Finally, where I have referred to, for example, a 12mm-diameter rope or 4mm long-link chain, that is how you buy it, and no conversion for Imperial feet and inches has been provided.

However, for other measurements, for example lengths of rope, both Imperial and metric measurements are included and have been rounded up or down, as appropriate. Feet and inches are shown as, for example 6'6" throughout; a metric conversion follows in square brackets, as a lower case m for metres and millimetres as mm.

All measurements are approximate as the stiffness and lay of the rope will alter the lengths required. If in doubt, it is always good policy to allow a little extra as no liability can be accepted if my guidelines and suggested lengths are not exact.

# Introduction

As a member of the International Guild of Knot Tyers, I have spent many years enjoying the pleasures of rope, string and cord, and the fascination of knots. So now I'd like to help you, the reader, get more pleasure and fun out of the ropes you deal with, while helping you become more accomplished and confident in rope handling.

As it says on the back cover, *Knots for the Cut* is aimed at narrowboat and cruiser owners the length and breadth of Britain's unique canal system and rivers, and other perfectionists. Although the knots in this book can apply to all types of boating, we are looking primarily at canal use.

One of the first hurdles a new boat owner will encounter is mooring the vessel, and I have covered this in some depth. Even before that, however, because the ropes themselves are as important as correct mooring, I have also included a small section on care and maintenance, and how to get the best from your expensive ropes and lines.

We then look in detail at the main knots canal and river boaters will need. Knots fall into two categories, permanent knots and temporary knots. Permanent knots are difficult to untie, such as the fisherman's knot, which is almost impossible to undo once it has been under tension.

On the other hand, hitches and bends need to be easy to undo, making them, of course, temporary. This book will clarify which is which, and the best uses for each of them.

I also want to encourage you to make your own fenders, both simple bottle fenders and, for the more ambitious, larger fenders for which you make a core and then cover it.

And finally, I have included some fancy ropework which you will enjoy making once you have mastered the basic knots. Cabin strings, tiller tassels and tingle buttons have a long tradition, being both useful and decorative. They have an interesting history too, which I have touched upon where appropriate.

The illustrations and text are deliberately large to aid clarity in the learning of these knots. Sizes and measurements given in this book are only an approximation. Experimentation is the best form of learning. Good luck, and enjoy many hours of twiddling fun.

*Ben Selfe*
*Knot Krazy*

CHAPTER 1

# Rope Maintenance

First of all, I'd like to deal with some of the ways rope can be damaged, and which can hasten its demise, but before that, a brief summary of the types of rope available today.

We can of course still get a limited supply of rope made from most of the natural fibres, including cotton, manila, hemp, sisal, coir, jute and a few others. All of these are becoming increasingly expensive and need special protection from the elements. Constant wet or damp would soon induce rot, mildew, even moss growth. Years ago, fenders would be immersed in creosote (now a banned substance) to help increase their lifespan.

Today there are many modern materials used for rope-making such as polypropylene, polyester, nylon, terylene and dynema. Types of rope include braid rope, braid on braid, braid on fibre, octiplait, hawser laid and cable laid, 3-strand and 4-strand rope, right-handed and left-handed laid rope, and probably several more I've never heard of.

But this is not a lesson in the history of rope or a discussion on modern rope manufacture. Rope has many enemies, the worst of which is the person who uses it. Just tying a bend or a hitch that is later undone has begun the damage caused by twisting, loosening, bending and stretching the very fibres of the rope. Running a rope over a pulley or a sheath has a similar effect. When a knot is no longer needed it should be removed from the rope as soon as possible.

At the end of the job in hand, the rope should be coiled in a kind and sympathetic manner, not just thrown into any old locker, especially when damp or wet, which will soon have it going mouldy, smelly and unpleasant to handle. If care is not taken when mooring to prevent or reduce chafing, the rope soon shows signs of fatigue. The next biggest enemy is dirt. Sand from the beach or building site, dust carried in the air, rope seems to be a magnet for grit and grime.

1

Clean ropes have a longer lifespan, so keeping them clean is important. Some detergents may damage natural fibres so simply rinse these in clean water and dry thoroughly by allowing air to pass freely around them.

On the other hand, modern man-made fibres will be fine on a low-temperature setting in the washing machine. Hank your rope before washing and place it in an old pillow case. Add mild detergent and softener, and dry in the same way as natural fibres.

Here follows some observations that will help you hank and store your rope in a sensible manner.

A lot of people coil a rope by wrapping it around thumb and elbow. This can force unwanted twists and kinks which will stay for long periods. It is much kinder to coil shorter lengths of rope no longer than about 33' [10m] loosely over one hand.

Twisting the rope as you go in the direction of the lay, coil it over your left hand. This method becomes fairly easy with a little practice, and ensures that the rope is not stored with unnatural or aggressive kinks or loosening of the lay.

Unfortunately, when uncoiled, rope can become tangled, caused by the twisting process when it was made, but not as aggressively as damage inflicted by the thumb and elbow method. Longer lengths of rope need to be flaked down using a figure-of-eight configuration.

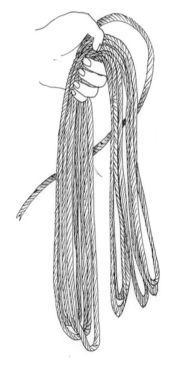

This helps the rope lay naturally and can be finished off using the same method as when coiled over the hand. Once fully flaked down, leaving a tail of about 4' [1.25m], pass your left hand under the centre of the figure-of-eight and pick up the whole hank.

Starting approximately 8 or 9" [200–230mm] down, pass the tail behind the hand and wrap it up neatly. When you have approximately 18" [460mm] of the tail left, form a loop and pass it through as you remove your left hand. The remaining tail is then passed through the single-strand loop and pulled snug. The hank is now ready to hang up.

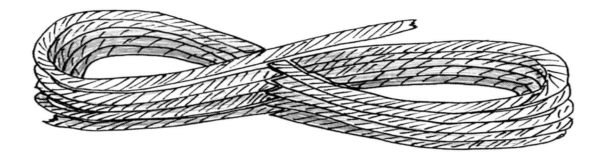

When you want to use rope that has been coiled in a figure-of-eight, the lashing should be untied and separated, and the hank placed back on the ground.

Try to arrange the hank back in a figure-of-eight with the tail uppermost, and you'll find it will pull off smoothly, with a lot less kinks or tangling.

# Before Mooring Your Boat

After 50 years of playing with boats of all types and sizes, one thing I have noticed over that time, that has remained glaringly consistent, is that most people have little or no idea how to moor their vessel. I have witnessed many a knot that could only be described as criminal.

I have also seen boats floating aimlessly in the middle of the harbour, that have come loose from their moorings due to ignorance and ineptitude on the part of the moorer.

In this chapter, with a few basic and simple knots, hitches and mooring methods, I hope to help novice boaters become competent enough to moor a boat securely and safely.

You will see that I have utilised some of the mooring etiquette that prevails throughout the sailing fraternity. As the number of boats on our inland waterways increases, sea-going methods and considerations become more appropriate for canal and river users too.

Remember it is good policy for both legal and security reasons to have the mooring line's final fastening on your boat, especially if you are in an area where you could be cast adrift by little darlings in the dead of night. A determined perpetrator might board your vessel which, at the very least, is trespass with intent, or better still, an act of piracy which, on the high seas, is still punishable by hanging!

# CHAPTER 2

# Mooring Your Boat

When it comes to securing your boat alongside, it is sometimes difficult to decide the best method. Is there a nearby bollard that could be used to take a round turn, bringing the line back to the boat, then belaying, using dolly, T-bar or cleat?

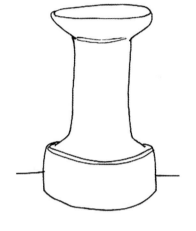

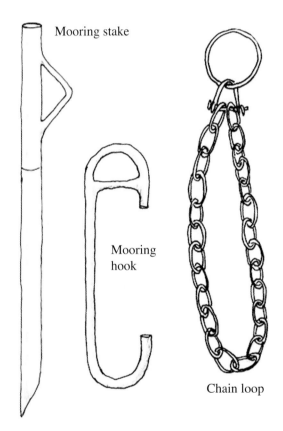

Mooring stake

Mooring hook

Chain loop

Or should it be passed through a chain loop, cow-hitched to a piling stringer, mooring hook or mooring stake? This is a decision you must make every time you moor your boat.

It is kinder on the rope to take a full round turn, as illustrated, rather than singly. This reduces chafe and increases the longevity of your mooring lines.

# Cow-hitching

Before we move on, it is worth mentioning the cow hitch, which is very useful in preventing premature chafing around dollies or T-bars.

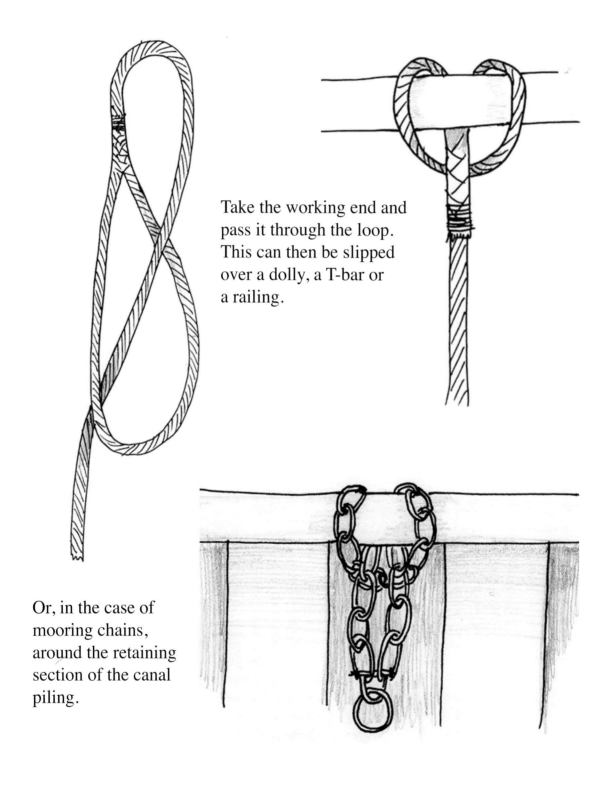

Take the working end and pass it through the loop. This can then be slipped over a dolly, a T-bar or a railing.

Or, in the case of mooring chains, around the retaining section of the canal piling.

# The Anchor Hitch
# or Fisherman's Bend

The Anchor Hitch, sometimes referred to as the Fisherman's Bend, is similar to a round turn and two half hitches (*see page 20*). The only difference is that the first half hitch is passed *under* the two round turns, and finished off with a further hitch on top.

The remaining working end can be passed under two or more lays of the standing part to make a nice neat and secure hitch. This can obviously only be done in a three-strand rope.

# Lighterman's Hitch

On narrowboats, most of us have dollies (small bollards) or T-bars. The best method for securing your boat is the lighterman's hitch. A clove hitch can be very difficult to untie once it has been tightened under tension. More about the clove hitch later.

Take a turn on the dolly or T-bar and remove the slack by tweaking, that is to say whilst maintaining a slight pull on the working end, drag up a bight between dolly and the shore. Then as the bight is released, pull the slack from the working end.

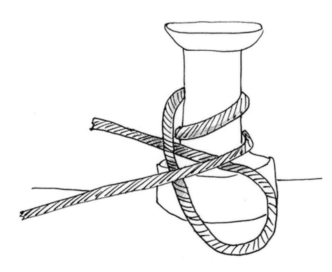

Now pass a loop under the shore-going line, adding a twist to bring the working end of the rope nearest the dolly.

Now pass the loop over the top of the dolly.

Work slack back to the working end to snug up.

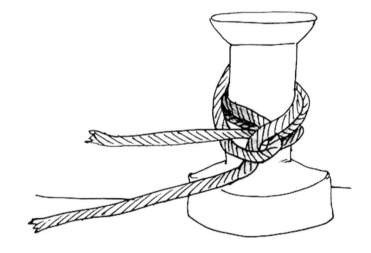

This method is all that's needed to secure the largest ocean liner, so I think it will be more than sufficient for your narrowboat or cruiser.

# Belaying on a T-bar or Cleat

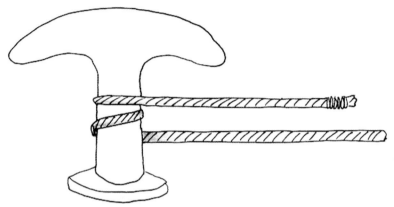

An alternative method of securing to a T-bar or cleat is to belay. This is achieved by passing a round turn around the T-bar.

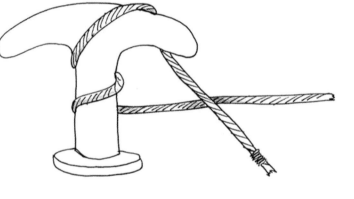

Pass the working end over the top of the T-bar and then under it.

Pass once again over the top, trapping the first over.

Using the fact that the mooring line is trapped, and very little slack can return down the line, make a loop, forming a figure-of-eight.

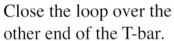

Close the loop over the other end of the T-bar.

Pull firmly to snug up.

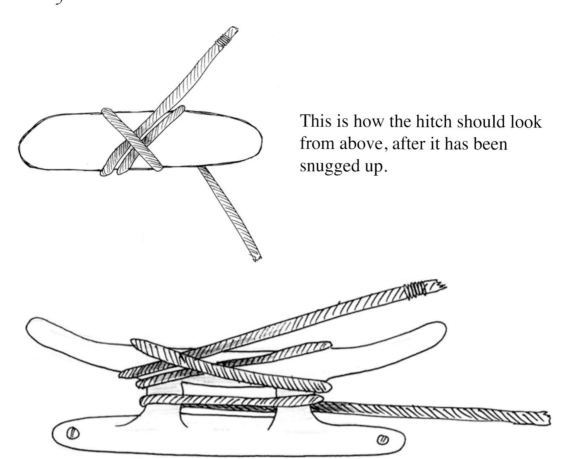

This is how the hitch should look from above, after it has been snugged up.

Should you have cleats on your boat, the belaying on a T-bar or cleat method can also be used to achieve the same effect.

# Cheesing Down

To finish off, short ends of rope left over after mooring are often neatly cheesed down. This can be accomplished by starting in the middle of the cheese with the bitter end.

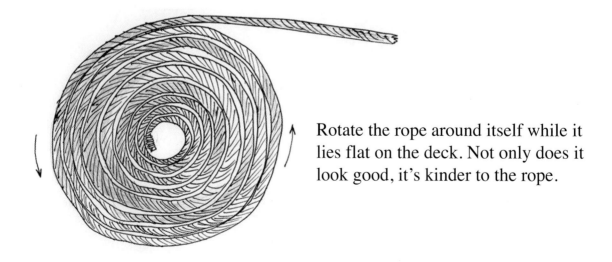

Rotate the rope around itself while it lies flat on the deck. Not only does it look good, it's kinder to the rope.

# Bowlines and Moorings

On occasion, it is necessary to place a loop over a bollard. The strongest knot, and the kindest to your rope, is probably the bowline. With a little practice this knot is quite simple to tie. I will tell it to you as it was taught to me at the age of nine.

First make a rabbit's hole . . .

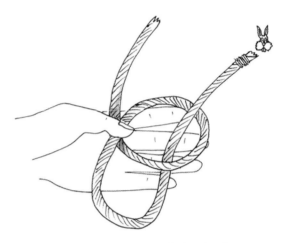

The rabbit comes out of the hole. . .

. . . sees me . . .

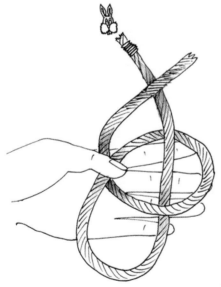

Rabbit runs behind the tree . . .

. . . and then dives back down into his hole again.

Now hold A and B in your right hand, take strand C in your left hand, and pull out the slack.

# Crowded Moorings

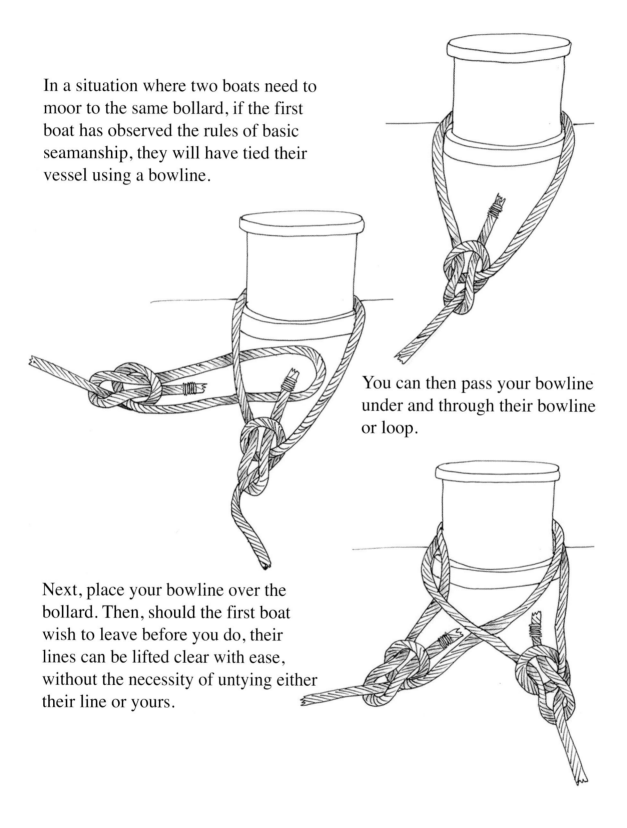

In a situation where two boats need to moor to the same bollard, if the first boat has observed the rules of basic seamanship, they will have tied their vessel using a bowline.

You can then pass your bowline under and through their bowline or loop.

Next, place your bowline over the bollard. Then, should the first boat wish to leave before you do, their lines can be lifted clear with ease, without the necessity of untying either their line or yours.

# Correct Mooring Procedures

On some occasions it may be necessary on canals and rivers, and always at sea, to moor your vessel using a stern line, breast ropes and springs. This is to prevent excessive movement, which could result in collisions with boats moored fore and aft. It will also assist in coping with the rise and fall of the tide.

This could of course require a loop made in the middle of a long mooring line, so that one rope can be used for two or more functions, for example, breast rope and spring. With narrowboats, we mainly use what can loosely be described as a cross between stern and bowline/breast rope.

Finally, always be aware of the rise and fall in tide or water levels, particularly on rivers. I have seen boats hanging by their lines from the harbour wall!

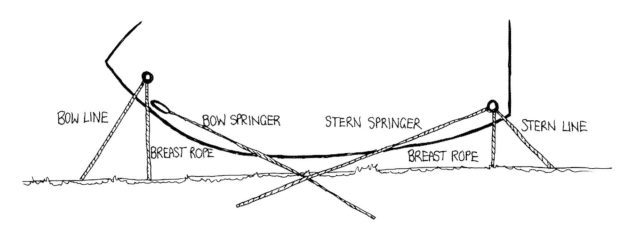

# Bowline on the Bight

Fold a bight in the rope approximately in the position where it will be needed. Be generous or you might end up with the working end too short to finish the knot or hitch.

Now using the doubled rope, proceed in a similar manner to tying an ordinary bowline. This time the bight is the rabbit.

The rabbit comes out of the hole . . .

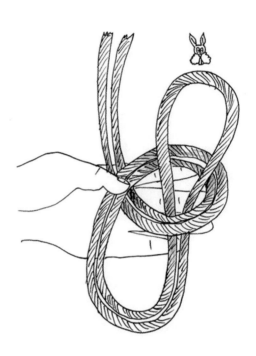

. . . but this time, instead of going round the tree, the bight must be opened.

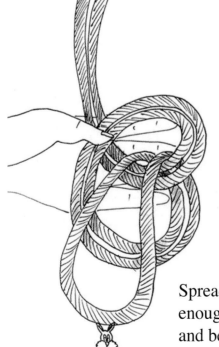

Spread the bight wide enough to pass under and behind.

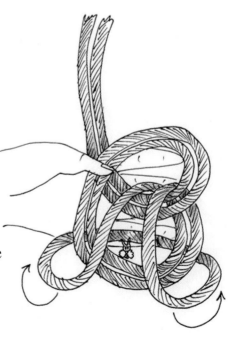

Bring the bight up behind the tree to its final position.

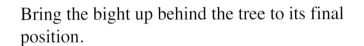

Pull the slack back into the loop. You now have one loop and two working ends.

You can now drop the loop over the bollard/T-bar. One working end can be used as a breast rope, bow or stern line, and the other working end as a spring.

# Round Turn and Two Half-Hitches

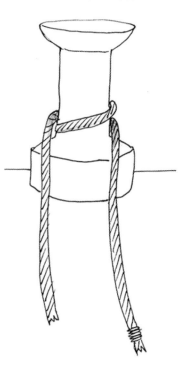

Take the working end of the bow or stern line from the vessel to the shore, then return to the dolly. Mooring your boat can now be finished off with a round turn and two half-hitches. Make a round turn on the dolly or T-bar, and remove slack in the working end.

Then make a simple hitch with the working end snugged up.

Now follow with a second simple hitch. Any spare line could be cheesed down in order to look tidy.

# Clove Hitch

On numerous occasions I have seen boats moored using a clove hitch. This is not recommended as it can become extremely tight once it has been under tension, and difficult to untie. If left loose, it has been known to work itself free. However, the knot is very useful for other applications and should be part of your repertoire.

Take a turn around your dolly or bollard, with the working end under.

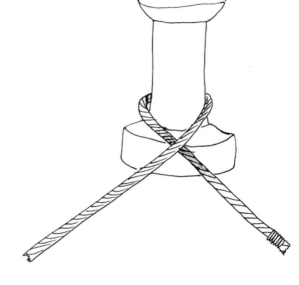

Pull up the slack to the working end and form a bight, then pass it over the dolly or bollard.

Now snug it up. The best use for a clove hitch is on your pennant staff to hoist your flag or possibly tying your fender lanyard to a rail.

# CHAPTER 3

# Joining Rope Together

There are many reasons why rope might need to be joined. When your mooring line is not long enough, or when a line breaks because of undue stress placed upon it. Sadly, I have seen already weakened rope joined together with an overhand knot.

This particular knot will weaken an already stressed rope, reducing its effectiveness almost to nil. This would definitely be considered a permanent knot. Should it be successfully tightened, it would be impossible to untie. The knot also stands a very good chance of 'capsizing' when under tension, thereby turning a stressed situation into a dangerous one.

## The Fisherman's Knot

Should you need to join together two pieces of similar-sized rope, a far better permanent knot would be a fisherman's knot, which is none other than two interlocking overhand knots tied over the working ends of both ropes.

Pull out slack and snug up. This is a far stronger knot and does not significantly weaken the rope. But the best way, if possible, is the straight splice, (*see page 32*).

# The Sheet Bend

The best method to temporarily join two pieces of rope, even of different thicknesses, would be the sheet bend. Take the thickest rope (A) and form a bight on the working end.

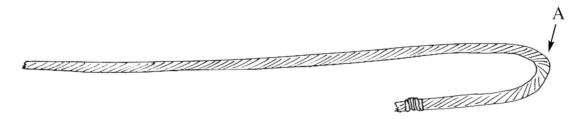

Place the working end of rope B under the bight, leaving sufficient length to complete the knot, about 8" [200mm], ensuring that B passes over the shortest part of A.

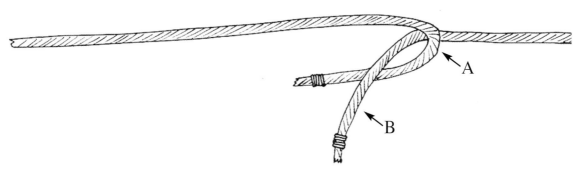

Pass rope B under both parts of rope A.

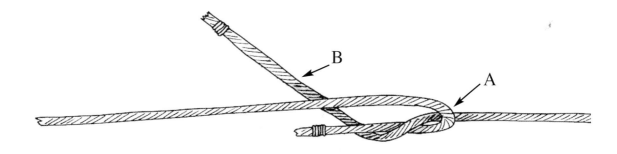

Close off by passing the working end of rope B through the loop formed between A and B.

Snugged up this makes an easily untied yet secure strong bend.

The pass in the centre can be doubled.

Once snugged up, this will produce an even more secure bend.

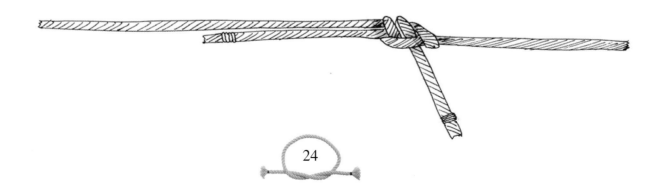

# CHAPTER 4

# Splicing and Whipping

## The Eye Splice

First we must decide how large a loop is required. Let's say we need a loop with a total length of 6" [150mm]. Let's also assume that we are using 12mm-diameter rope. Place a temporary whipping 8" [200mm] from one end and a further temporary whipping 12" [300mm] further down. This could be a tape whipping as it is only used as a guide and to prevent unnecessary unlaying of the rope. Unlay the working end and separate the strands, taping each one to prevent the individual fibres from unlaying.

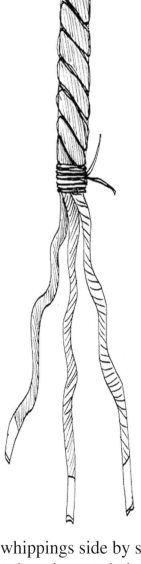

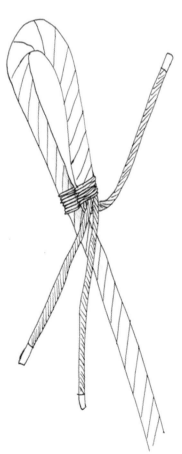

Place the two whippings side by side and ensure that there is no twisting of the rope as this will make an unnatural and uncomfortable loop. Place two strands either side of the fall of rope.

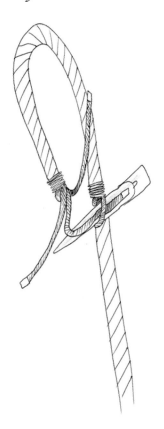

Always start a splice with the centre strand. Twist the fall of the rope to unlay and insert your Swedish fid as close as possible to the whipping. Feed the centre strand into the fid and through the hole you have made.

Pull the slack through, snug but not too tight, twisting the strand to tighten the lay as you go. This is called a tuck.

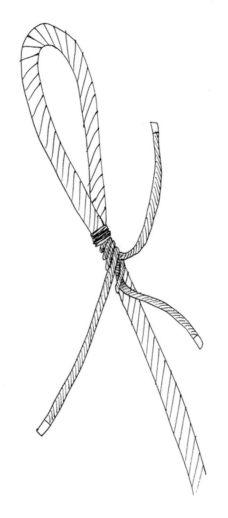

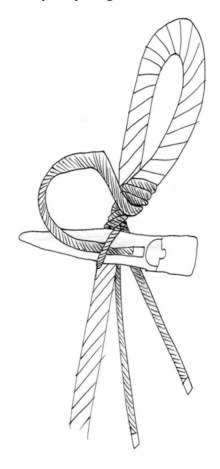

The next strand to tackle is what I call the dog's leg. Looking down on your work and assuming this is right-hand-laid rope, this will be on the left-hand-side of your splice. Slightly turn the rope anti-clockwise, open the next strand of rope with the fid and tuck in the dog's leg strand.

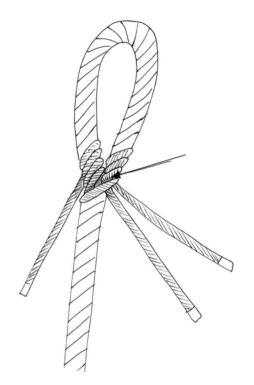

You will notice that, when snugged up, this strand changes direction. Twist the work 180° clockwise and tuck in the remaining strand. Check that there is a strand coming out from between each strand of the fall and that all are as near to the whipping as possible.

If this is not the case, I suggest you remove all three and start again. Give each one a final twist and snug up, and repeat the procedure.

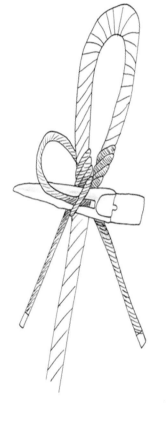

Four sets of tucks is normal but this should be increased to five on polypropylene rope and six on nylon rope. Should you be splicing polyprop or nylon, don't forget to allow extra rope for tucking. You can now remove the temporary tape whippings. To finish the eye splice properly, you should whip the strands back to the fall. This can be achieved with a simple whipping, (*see page 35*).

# Back Splice

By forming a loop for the eye splice, you have ensured that the strands are heading in the right direction for splicing. Unfortunately, this is not the case with a back splice. So we have to devise a method to send the strands in the correct direction. This is achieved by forming a crown with the parted strands. For a piece of 12mm-diameter rope, approximately 6 or 7" [150–180mm] of rope will be needed to give four passes and have enough remaining to whip and finish.

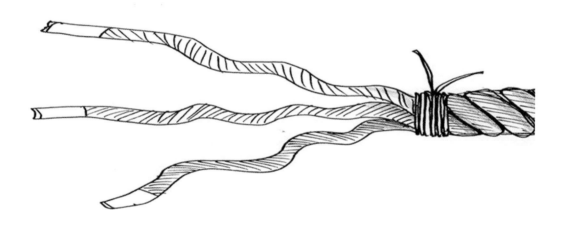

## Forming a Crown

Tie a lashing 6–7" [150–180mm] from the end of the rope and partially unlay sufficient rope and tightly bind the top of each strand. Masking tape is ideal for this purpose. Once each strand has been taped to prevent it from unravelling, open the rope as far back as the whipping.

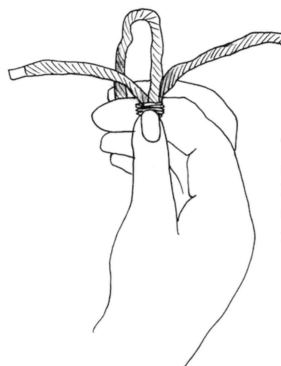

Taking the middle strand facing you and hidden under your thumb, pass it between the two remaining strands and hold in a loose loop with your finger on the far side of the rope.

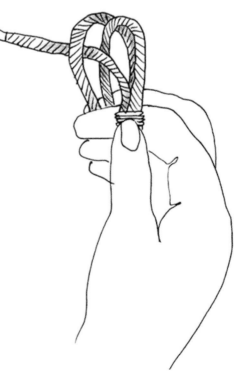

Taking the right-hand strand, pass it in front of the remaining strand and hold it down to the right of that strand.

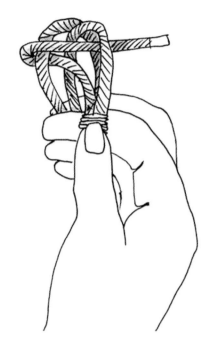

The remaining strand sticking up in the air can now be pushed through the original loop, forming a crown.

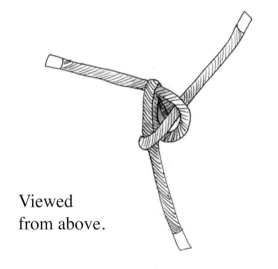

Viewed from above.

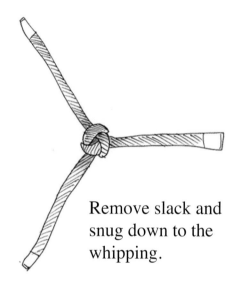

Remove slack and snug down to the whipping.

Remove the tape whipping. Using a Swedish fid, pass under any strand, starting from where the whipping has been removed.

Taking the strand that lies
immediately behind the pointed end
of the fid, pass it under the next
strand. That is to say, the strand
leaves the crown, goes over one
strand and under the strand where
the fid has been placed.

Follow the same sequence
with strands 2 and 3. After
it has been twisted to
remake the strands (as in
the eye splice), it should
look like this.

Repeat this process a further three times, twisting and
pulling up to the previous tuck as you go.

# Straight Splice

The straight splice is probably the most secure way of joining two ropes together. It can certainly be described as permanent. Most mooring lines are made of 3-strand rope in one guise or another. Some of course are made of braid on braid, usually seen on modern cruisers. Splicing braid on braid is fraught with difficulty in inexperienced hands since it needs several measurements and calculations.

Here we will concentrate on the basic 3-strand method. It is stronger than tying a bowline.

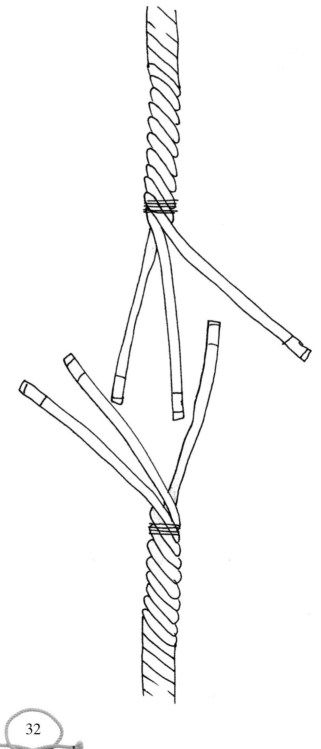

For a 12–16mm rope, place a whipping (a constrictor knot is ideal, *see page 59*) 6–8" [150–200mm] from each end of the ropes to be joined. Unlay the rope as far as the whipping and tape the ends with masking tape.

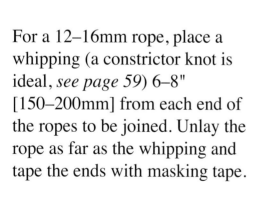

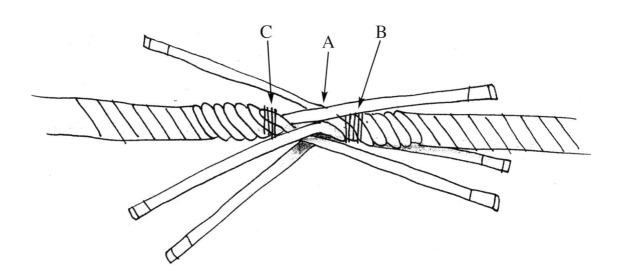

Interlock and marry the strands together. A further whipping at A is useful but not absolutely necessary. It would hold the strands back to the rope.

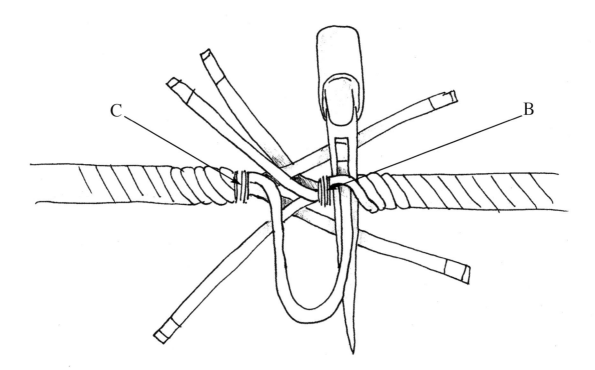

Break the lay of the rope by twisting. Starting with any of the strands, insert the fid as close to the whipping as possible, *as shown*, ensuring that each strand locks over its neighbour. Once the first tuck has been completed, whipping B should be removed. Then remove any slack.

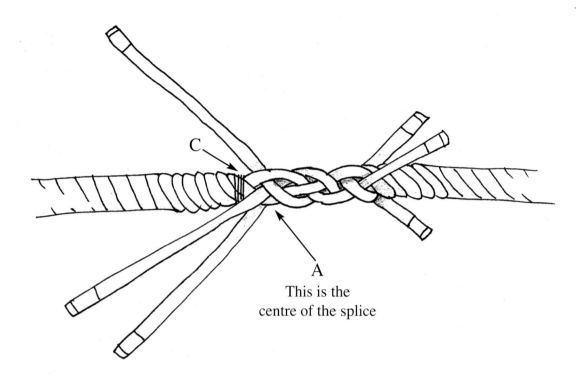

A
This is the
centre of the splice

Now that the whipping at B has been
removed, you can tighten and
continue for three rows of tucks.

If you made a whipping at A, remove
it and the original whipping C, and
repeat tucking on the other side of the
centre of the splice. You will then
have six tucks in all.

# Simple Whipping

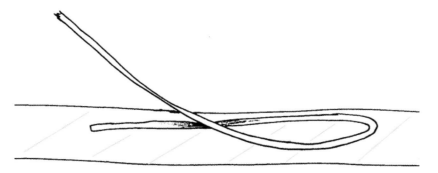

Now we've mastered splicing, we need to learn straightforward whipping. It looks good if the last strands of your splice are whipped back to the fall of the rope. It also aids the security of the splice. With a length of whipping twine, form a loop and lay it parallel to the item to be covered. We have chosen to show this on rope but it could be used for such things as replacing the eyes on a fishing rod or holding something together, for example a split broom handle. The simple whipping has many uses.

Pass the working end of your whipping twine twice behind and around, trapping the loop.

Continue wrapping around until the desired length is achieved, pulling each round as tightly as possible.

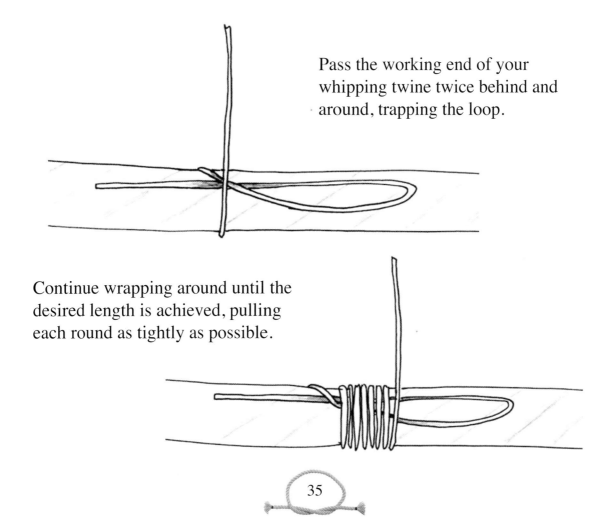

Pass the working end of the whipping twine through the loop, maintain tension on the working end and pull the other end tight until all is hidden under the whipping.

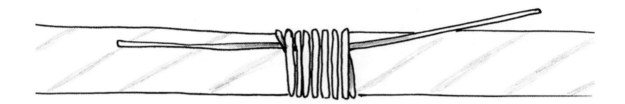

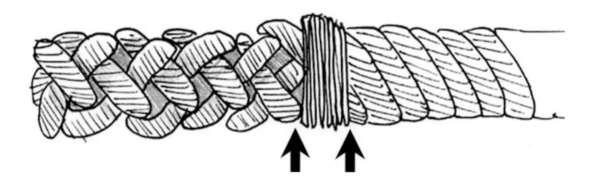

Carefully cut off the surplus ends of the whipping twine, and tuck out of sight.

CHAPTER 5

# Turk's Heads for Tillers or Tables

Turk's Heads have several uses. They can be mounted on a tiller bar so that it doesn't damage the painted roof of your boat when you rest it there. They are also useful as a natural rain drip to stop water entering the rudder stock on a butty boat.

They were sometimes used to make a repair on a split shaft or spar, and to strengthen the rudder stock on the butty, which was prone to splitting at the head. A Turk's Head was more attractive than whipping in such a visible place.

Other uses include as an extra grip on such items as boat hooks or barge poles, which again would protect the painted roof when placed upon it, where it was decorative and a nice place to show off your handiwork.

I have found many uses for Turk's Heads, and there are hundreds of designs and styles to choose from. So many, in fact, that there are several books on the market that deal with Turk's Heads alone.

We will only talk here of the three most useful Turk's Heads. My favourite use is for adding strength and sacrificial decoration to my fenders, especially buttons, dwarf's trousers and barge fenders. And although not technically a Turk's Head, by popular request I've included an ocean plait mat.

# Practice String

For Turk's Heads, I always use a practice string. You will need to practise tying and un-tying until you get it right. I suggest you use a 6–8' [2–2½m] length of fairly stiff braided 6mm rope. It will enable you to practise many knots, and Turk's Heads in particular, until you can do them without looking at the diagrams. Practice makes perfect!

# Four Three Turk's Head

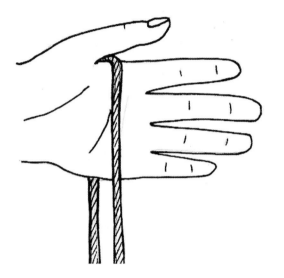

1. To make this Turk's Head, you will need a piece of 6mm rope measuring 8' [2.5m] long. Start half way along and place it between your left-hand thumb and index finger so that it falls across your palm.

2. Using the working end, pass it from the palm to the back of the hand between the second and third fingers.

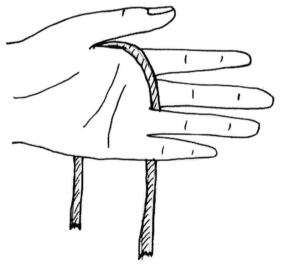

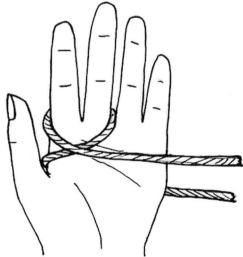

3. Bringing the working end between thumb and first finger, cross the bight over the palm.

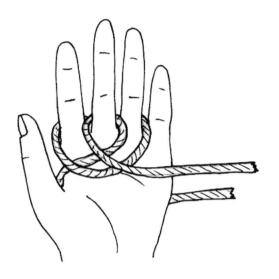

4. Hold at the point where it crosses with the thumb and form a new bight between your ring and little fingers, returning between your first and second fingers to cross the first bight.

5a. Remove the shorter end from behind the thumb and pass under the working end that you have just released, and replace over the thumb.

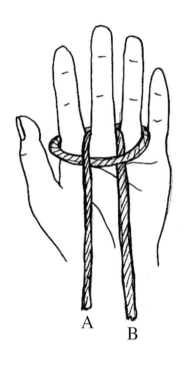

A    B

5b. Firstly cross working end B over working end A, and trap between thumb and fore finger.

Now study what you have, and you will see you have the opportunity to weave a ladder along the first crease of your fingers.

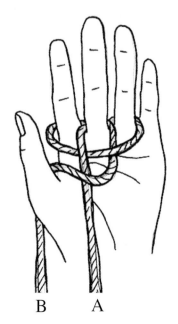

B    A

6. Take working end A and, starting from the right, pass it along the first crease of the fingers with an over, then under, repeat the over then under again, and weave the working end through. Pull this through until all three bights are approximately the same size.

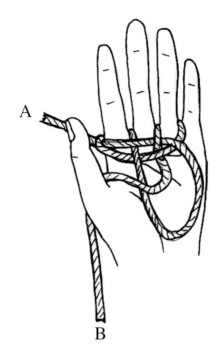

7. Now remove from your hand and adjust to a cloverleaf pattern to make a mat. If you want to make a tiller Turk's Head, go to the next page.

8. You then follow with the working end on the inside of the first fall around to double it. Then, using the remainder of the rope, treble it.

9. Adjust until the ends meet at opposing lays of the rope where the ends can now be sewn together on the underside of the mat. (*See page 54 for a photograph of this final step.*)

# Four Three Turk's Head for Tiller

10. Follow the directions as for the mat (1–7), but instead of making a cloverleaf, remove the knot gently from your hand and make it into a cylinder, adjusting individual strands and making sure it is open enough to fit over the tiller with plenty of room to spare. This is important because the knot will tighten significantly when the second and third passes are made. If you don't have enough cord to finish trebling, don't panic.

11. The knot can then be placed on the tiller and tightened by working through the slack to either of the free ends. This slack can then be used to complete the trebling. If you find you don't have quite enough rope to treble at this stage, PANIC! Make sure you pull the last strand from your previous tuck through and under the Turk's Head, and that it is completely tight before cutting off the loose ends and hiding the cut cord out of sight.

# Five Three Turk's Head

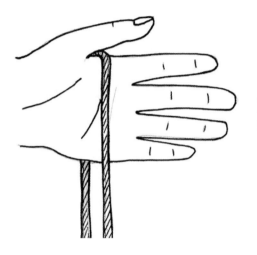

1. Again using your practice cord, place the centre of the rope across the palm of your left hand.

2. Taking the fall from behind, wind it twice around your hand. You now have three bights around the hand.

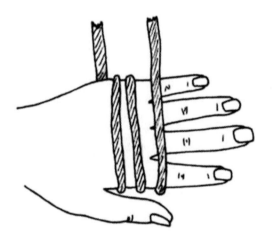

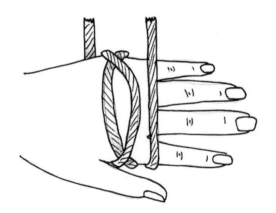

3. Working from the back of the hand, take the bight furthest to the left, bring it across over the centre bight to form a ladder.

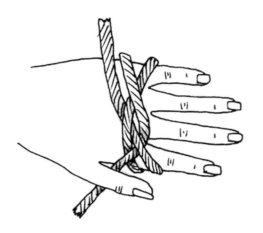

4. Lock off using the working end (the strand on the right). Weave as in English three-strand plaiting.

5. Turn your hand so the palm is facing you again, and lock off with the working end.

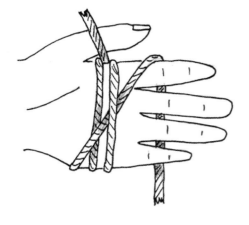

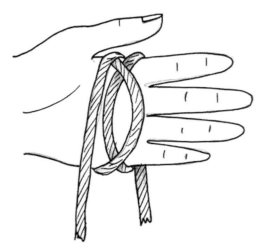

6. Take the centre bight and place it over the left bight to form a new ladder.

43

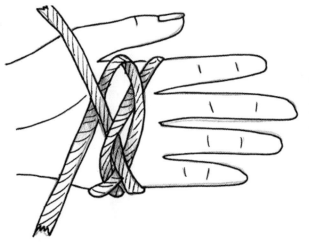

7. Lock off using the working end. You now have a five-bight Turk's Head. At this point we must decide whether it is for the tiller or the table.

8. First we will tackle the tiller. For this we will once again have to form a cylinder, and use both ends to double then treble. As I said previously, if you don't have enough cord to finish trebling, don't panic.

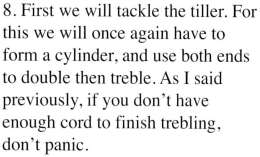

9. The knot can then be placed on the tiller and tightened by working through the slack to either of the free ends. This slack can then be used to complete the trebling. Make sure you pull the last strand from your first tuck through and under the Turk's Head and that it is as tight as possible before cutting off loose ends and hiding the cut cord out of sight.

Once we have practised the Five Three Turk's Head, using the same principle and larger loops, this Turk's Head can go up in increments of two bights. By adding further crosses forming ladders, and locking off using the working end, a Three Nine Turk's Head will enhance the look of buttons or dwarf's trousers, and add strength to the point where the chain leaves the fender.

At the opposite end of the scale, you can replace the rope with cord, and a Three Nine Turk's Head makes a nice bracelet.

# Five Three Turk's Head as a Mat

10. If you want to make the Turk's Head as a mat, return to number 7 on the previous page, remove the knot from your hand, and place it on a flat surface.

11. Double and treble as above, making sure that when the mat is finished the rope can be cut and sewn so that the ends are concealed under an opposing set of bights.
(*See page 54 for a photograph of this final step.*)

# Five Four Turk's Head

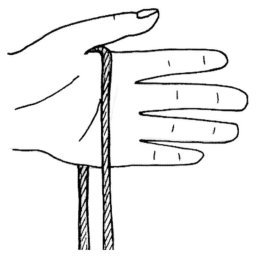

1. This Turk's Head is a superior cylindrical or flat mat, but is a little more complicated than the others. Using a practice cord, place over your left hand so that you have an equal fall to the front and rear. That is to say, half way!

2. With your palm facing you, take the rear strand and tie a thumb knot going over then under the front strand.

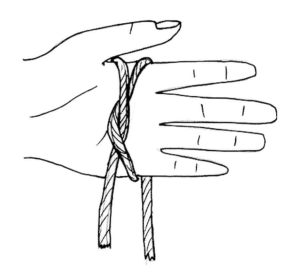

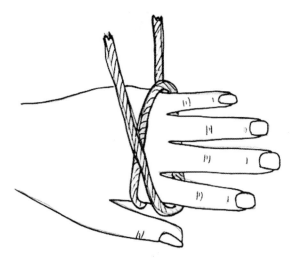

3. Turn your hand palm down and place the working end over the remaining strand.

4. Applying a little tension to the working end, turn your hand back to its original position. The working end should now look as shown here. I find it easier at this stage to place the working end temporarily under my thumb.

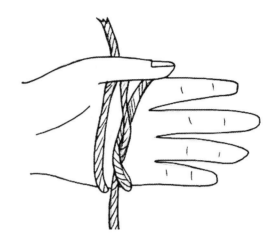

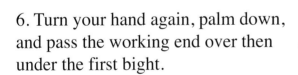

5. Pass the working end under and through the ladder that has been formed.

6. Turn your hand again, palm down, and pass the working end over then under the first bight.

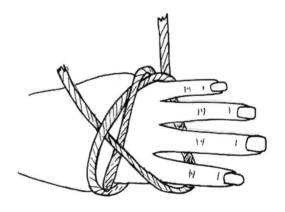

7. Support the working end of the rope with your thumb and index finger, and turn the hand palm up.

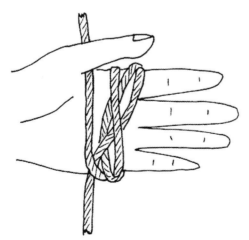

8. This time ensure that the working end emerges from the left of your hand, and passes over the fall of the rope. Move the working end under the thumb and stretch the original crossing apart to form a ladder. Then with the working end, lock off.

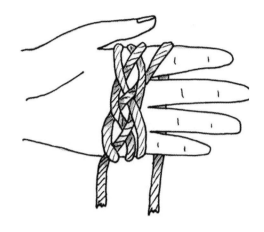

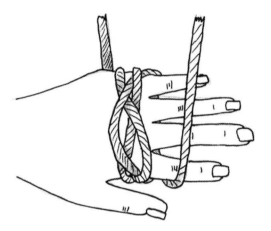

9. Slide the Turk's Head down your fingertips to release some of the tension, and the final ladder lies on top of the fingers.

10. Pass the working end over, under, and over, and work the slack through gently to form a tidy, cylindrical shape.

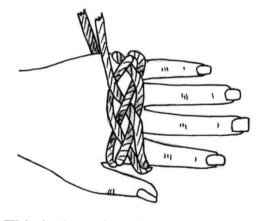

11. This is the point where we must once again decide whether we want a cylinder or a mat. My personal opinion is that this Turk's Head is difficult to tighten as a mat, and is perhaps not best suited for this purpose. At this stage, the cylinder would be doubled and trebled.

12. The knot can then be placed on the tiller and tightened by working through the slack to either of the free ends. Make sure you pull the last strand from your last tuck through and under the Turk's Head and that it is completely tight before cutting off loose ends and hiding the cut cord on the wrong side of the finished Turk's Head.

13. If you want to make the Turk's Head into a mat, remove from your hand, place on a flat surface and flatten as shown.

14. Double and treble, making sure that when the mat is finished, the rope can be cut and sewn to conceal the ends under an opposing set of bights. (*See page 54 for a photograph of this final step.*)

*The five-pass ocean plait mat. Using different sizes of rope, it can be made to any size, either as a table mat or as a door mat.*

# The Ocean Plait Mat

The ocean plait mat can be used for several useful purposes aboard your vessel, or even in the home. For a good bulky door mat, it will take approximately 90' [27m] of 14–16mm diameter rope – manilla is perfect for this. At the other end of the scale, 33' [10m] of 6mm diameter manilla makes an excellent centre mat for the table, or a galley mat for hot saucepans. It is also a worthwhile exercise in knot tying, and very rewarding.

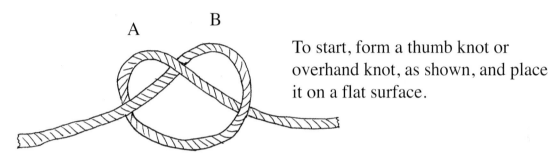

To start, form a thumb knot or overhand knot, as shown, and place it on a flat surface.

Elongate the top loops to form rabbit's ears.

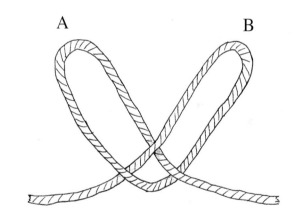

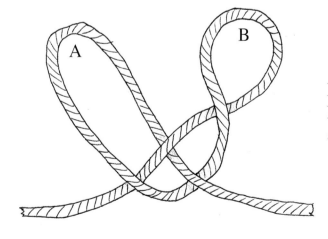

Lift the right-hand bight at B, half twist in a clockwise direction, and place as shown.

Take strand A, also half twist clockwise, and place across the loose bight formed with strand B.

Taking the left-hand working end, pass if over A, completely under both strands of loop B.

Now take the right-hand working end, pass it under the strand at C, and lock off the ladder, that is, over, under, over and under.

Now you can make the final loop. Take the left-hand strand and run it parallel to the other working strand, using up one length at a time. Then continue doubling, trebling or, as I have done, making five passes altogether. Make sure all the loops are in a tidy position, and not too tightly drawn through so that the strands can be doubled, trebled, etc., without causing it to distort.

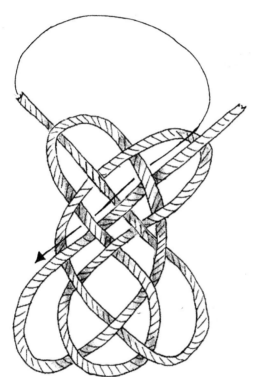

It is a lot easier to keep the work loose and then tighten after all passes are made. Keep your work loose, making every bight bigger than you need, *then* tighten a little at a time in order to reclaim sufficient length to complete. If you make it too tight too soon, it will easily distort.

When you are happy with the final shape, dimensions, etc., and it is pleasing to the eye, turn it over so that the wrong side is facing you. Thread your needle with twine, and go through the first strand you are intending to sew, passing the needle from the inside. Do not pull the twine right through, but first wrap it two or three times around the rope end, then pass the needle through from the outside. Repeat with the other end. (*See photo overleaf*).

This is the reverse side of your ocean plait mat, and shows how to secure and hide the ends out of sight. This avoids the danger of their coming loose and allowing the work to unravel.

# CHAPTER 6

# Making Your Own Fenders

Making your own fenders may seem daunting at first, but don't despair, you will find it fairly easy with a little practice. The art of fender making is relatively simple because there are only a few knots to learn in order to make attractive and practical fenders.

In this chapter we are going to talk about side fenders, also known as bottle fenders. I am going to give you detailed instructions on how to make just one of the styles of bottle fender I make, with a choice of how to finish it, either the standard two crowns or the doubled footrope method.

A major point to consider is the type of rope to use. Synthetic fibres such as polypropylene are available in many colours, although black is probably the most practical as lighter colours will soon show the dirt. Synthetic hemp (also a polypropylene) makes a very attractive fender. Polyprop fenders have the added benefit of floating, should they break free and fall into the water.

It must be remembered that the rope you choose or have available will vary the shape, size and overall appearance of the finished article. The best rope to use is probably end-of-life mooring lines, halyards, etc. Older rope is easier to tie and looks more natural. Unfortunately, I seem to be last in the queue when boat owners discard this valuable commodity.

Natural fibres look very attractive but sadly do not last too long, even when they are impregnated with preservatives. These natural fibres could include sisal, hemp, even cotton, although cotton would be very expensive and soon get dirty. Cotton fenders look nice in show conditions.

The other main point to consider is the final size. I show here a six-strand polypropylene fender made in 12mm-diameter rope. This should produce a fender a little over 3¼" [85mm] in diameter. After use this will reduce to approximately 2½–3" [65–75mm], an ideal size to use when cruising the canals. Anything larger will definitely get in the way when entering a lock.

In fact, travelling and entering locks with side fenders down is not a good policy. They can catch on entry, on loose bricks in the lock, or on exiting. Fenders should really only be used when you are moored in order to prevent chafing and banging, or between two vessels moored side by side.

# Tools you will need for fender-making

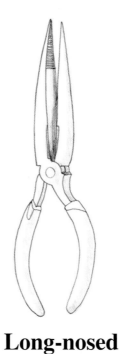

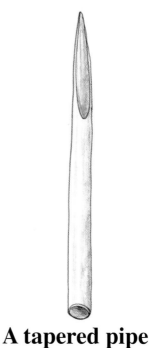

## Swedish Fid
Commercially available. Necessary for the Footrope finish

## Long-nosed Pliers
Commercially available. Absolutely necessary for making your fender.

## A tapered pipe
Not commercially available but needed for the standard finish. To make your own, you will need a 12" [300mm] stainless steel tube or similar-strength tubing with an inside diameter just large enough for the rope you are using to slide through easily. Cut off 2–2½" [50–65mm] at an acute angle, making sure all rough edges are removed with a file.

## Needle
Commercially available. A carpet needle, curved and slightly fanned out before tapering to a point. For sewing rope cores.

You will also need a soft-faced hammer, heavy-duty whipping twine and a sharp knife. An Opinel is the ideal knot-tyer's knife as it holds its edge for longer.

# Knots you will need to know for fender-making

Grocer's Hitch

Constrictor knot

Crown knot + Wall knot = Footrope Knot

Blanket stitch

These are the basic knots you need to learn, and knowing them will enable you to make all the fenders and some fancy ropework found in this book.

# Practice String

Almost every knot tyer you meet has a practice string in his pocket, ready to twiddle and fiddle at virtually any and every opportunity. I suggest you too carry a piece of fairly stiff braided 6mm rope. It will enable you to practise many of these knots until you can do them without looking at the diagrams. Practice makes perfect!

# The Grocer's Hitch

Before we start tying a fender, we need a method of whipping several ropes tightly together. The Grocer's Hitch is probably the easiest and best method to use.

Form a bight in the centre of a piece of very heavy twine approximately 20" [510mm] in length.

Pass the working end behind the fall and cross over itself.

Now pass the working end through the first bight and pass to tuck in alongside the fall of the twine.

Tighten the knot by stretching the twine apart at points A and B.

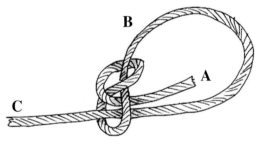

Now the loop can be doubled and if necessary enlarged to enable it to slide over your work and can be tightened by pulling at C.

# The Constrictor Knot

The constrictor knot is a self-trapping overhand knot that, once tightened securely, seldom loosens and is difficult to untie. This makes it ideal as a temporary whipping for splicing, etc. No attempt should be made to tie this knot around a finger as it will stop circulation and need to be cut off. (The knot, not the finger!) I therefore avoid teaching this knot to children.

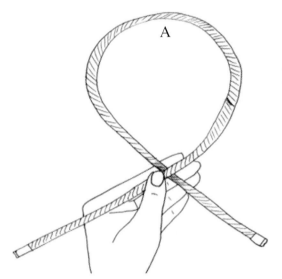

Form a bight in the centre of a 20" [510mm] piece of heavy twine. If you are right-handed, hold in the left hand. Pinch at A with thumb and forefinger of right hand. Now twist a quarter turn anti-clockwise. This will form two loops.

This is what it should look like from above. Now holding the centre at point A with thumb and forefinger of right hand, push the two loops down and under.

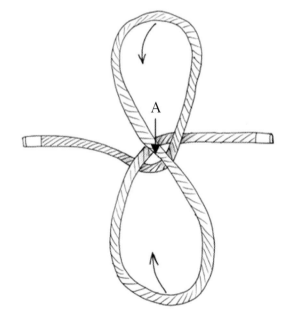

Tweak until both loops are even and if you look beneath the top strand you will see an overhand knot.

Once passed over your work, strands A and B can be rolled over your pointed-nose pliers and pulled very tight.

# Making a Bottle Fender

The first step to making a bottle fender is measuring and cutting the amount of rope needed. Using 12mm rope, cut three lengths 13' [4m] long. This will make a fender 20" [510mm] total length with a body circumference of around 3" [75mm]. Fold each of these lengths in half to double them.

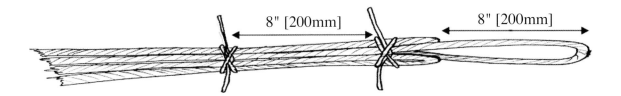

Arrange the three doubled pieces of rope and form a loop with the middle strand. Securely fasten with a whipping in the form of either a constrictor knot or a grocer's hitch, as shown in the diagram above. (*See pages 58 and 59*).

Holding the work by the top loop, select the two shorter strands and double them back up to the loop. Hold these strands out of the way with your non-writing hand.

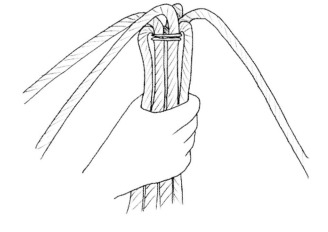

To form a crown round your core, take one of the remaining strands and call it strand number 1. Pass this strand to form a loop over its neighbour (strand 2) and hold back between your first and second finger. You may work either clockwise or anti-clockwise, the end result will be the same.

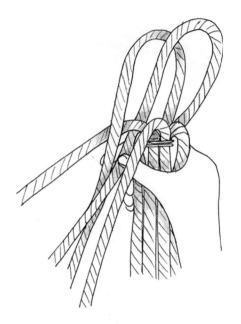

Take strand 2 and form a loop over strand 3 and once again hold back between first and second finger.

Repeat again with strand 3 over strand 4.

Pass strand 4 through the loop made with strand 1.

Remove all slack and tighten as much as possible.

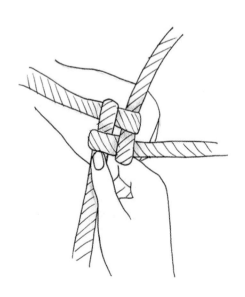

Now take the other two strands and place as near as possible to match the diagram, *right*, making sure there are two strands coming from under the crown, *as shown*, and that the crown has been tightened as much as possible to the whipping. Check the whipping and crown to make sure they haven't been loosened by this final manoeuvre.

Working with the loop uppermost – some people like to hang the work from a hook at this point – take strand 1 and place it between strands 2 and 3 to form a loop, making sure that you are going in the opposite direction to the way that it left the first crown. In other words, going back on itself.

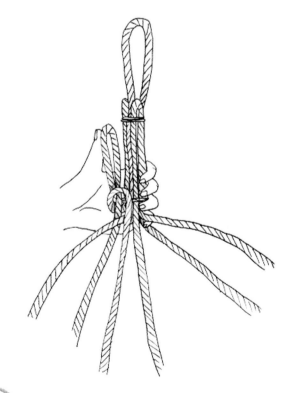

Take strand 2 and place it over the top of strand 3. This time the loop can be kept smaller. Continue round in the same fashion as before, passing strand 6 through the loop of strand 1.

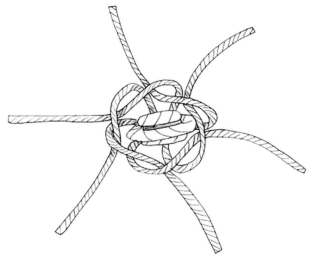

Viewed from above, and before tightening, your fender should look like this. This is an over-one crown knot. If there is a mistake at this stage, it is usually easier to untie to the previous stage and start again.

Changing direction again, repeat the process a further seven times, or until a tightened crown is level with the top of the added strands, as seen below. Make sure you have changed direction each time a full crown is completed. Make sure all the slack has been removed from each stitch or pass, pulling your work as tightly as possible.

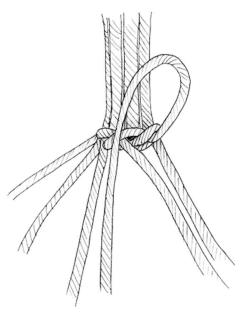

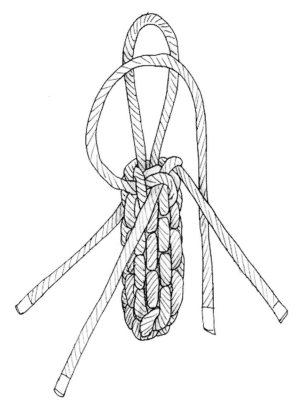

At this stage it is imperative that all stitches are tight and any slack should be worked through the fender using your pointed-nose pliers. Take the first stitch as it leaves the first crown, pulling as much slack as possible and work this slack through to the top of the fender. Repeat with the other five strands until all slack has been taken up. Check that the last row of crowns has reached the top, and covers the whipped loops so that the next row of crowns sits closely to the main loop.

The body of the fender is then finished off with an over-two crown knot. The number of over-two crowns depends on the finish you choose. If this is your first attempt at bottle fenders, a simple finish is probably best.

Therefore, three or four over-two crowns are required, depending on how well you've removed the slack. If you're brave enough to try the footrope finish (*see page 67*), the body will have to be reduced by one row.

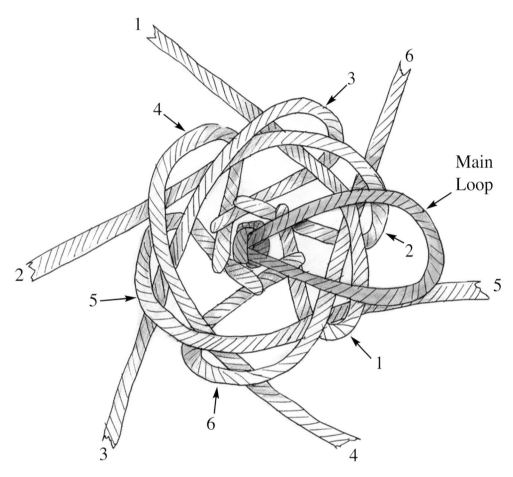

Making over-two crowns doubles the inside mass of rope and tightens its grip on the loop, which helps to prevent the fender turning inside out or slipping down and bunching at the bottom.

Take strand 1, once again in the opposite direction of flow, and pass it over strands 2 and 3. Take strand 2 and pass it over strands 3 and 4. Take strand 3 and pass it over strands 4 and 5. Strand 4 over 5 and 6. Strand 5 will pass over strand 6 and through the loop made by strand 1. Strand 6 will pass through the loops made by strands 1 and 2, taking care that this strand passes under all strands and loops previously made.

# Standard Finish

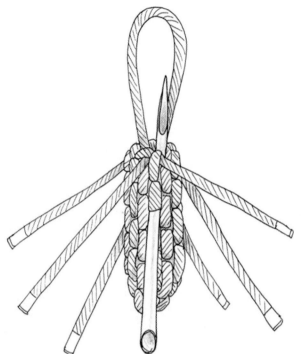

Making sure that all the slack has been removed from the over-two crowns, pass your tapered pipe (*as described on page 56*) through the outside stitches just above where the doubled strands were whipped to the core. Travel up the core to come out through the top of the body. *Note: The length of the body has been reduced to fit this page and should show 13 or 14 stitches.*

Work out which strand on the top would look the neatest to pull through. This is usually not the next stitch but the one after. Make sure that it is inserted far enough down the pipe to clear the body of the fender. Then remove the pipe.

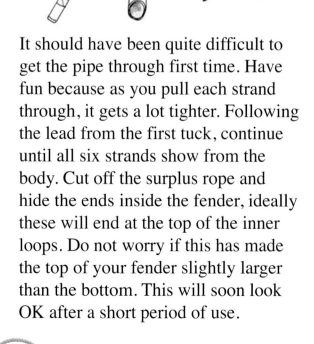

It should have been quite difficult to get the pipe through first time. Have fun because as you pull each strand through, it gets a lot tighter. Following the lead from the first tuck, continue until all six strands show from the body. Cut off the surplus rope and hide the ends inside the fender, ideally these will end at the top of the inner loops. Do not worry if this has made the top of your fender slightly larger than the bottom. This will soon look OK after a short period of use.

# The Footrope Finish

I hope by now you are brave enough to tackle the footrope finish. I think the footrope finish adds a lot to the decorative nature of the fender, and if tied properly, adds to the security of the finished fender too. It can be pulled extremely tight, which grips the loop and core more efficiently. Take your time and proceed carefully, it may be necessary to untie the knot several times and start again, but it is well worth the effort in the end. Follow the instructions until thirteen full stitches have been made around the core. Providing you have kept all the stitches as tight as possible, you should have around 6" [150mm] of loop remaining.

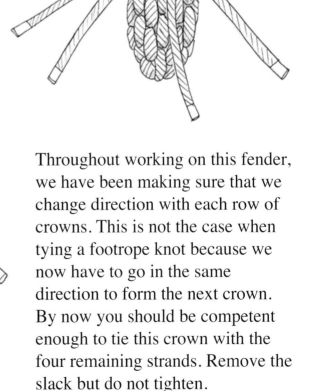

Select the two shortest strands, these should be on opposite sides of the loop. Keep them out of the way by lashing them up, making sure that at least 3" [75mm] is left clear between your last stitches and the whipping.

Throughout working on this fender, we have been making sure that we change direction with each row of crowns. This is not the case when tying a footrope knot because we now have to go in the same direction to form the next crown. By now you should be competent enough to tie this crown with the four remaining strands. Remove the slack but do not tighten.

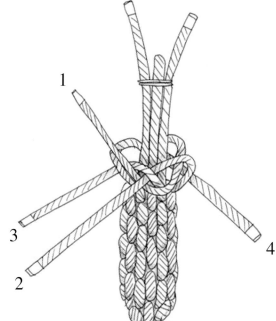

We are now going to tie an upside-down, back-to-front crown. This is called a wall knot. Take strand 1, pass under strand 2 to lay on top of strand 3, and follow round with strands 2 and 3.

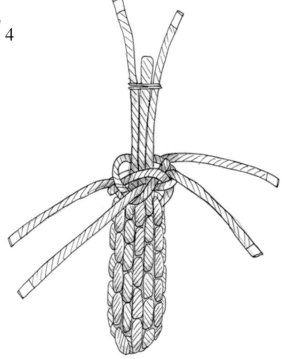

Strand 4 will now pass under and through the loop made in strand 1. This may be slightly confusing so be careful and then check that each strand appears in the same place all the way round. If it doesn't, it is probably best to untie the wall and crown knots, and start again.

In the International Guild of Knot Tyers, we have a saying, "First you crown and then you wall, follow it round and that is all."

Making sure that your working strands lay on the top, you can now follow the strand underneath. You will need to pass strand 1 under the strand 1 loop made in the first crown. The next strand will follow the same pattern, i.e. the loop made by itself as it leaves the main body of the fender.

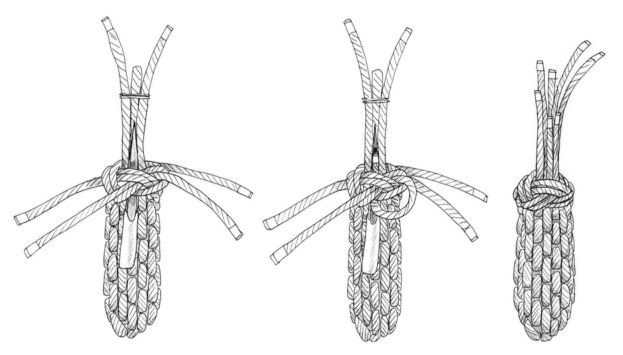

Now each strand needs to be tucked through the centre of the footrope knot to lay parallel to the loop. A Swedish fid or your cut pipe would be good for this purpose.

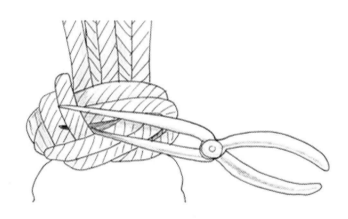

Using your pointed-nose pliers, work slack through by twisting the pliers. Do not try to take too much at a time as this can cause the symmetry of the footrope knot to distort.

You are better taking several small bites until the footrope knot is rock hard.

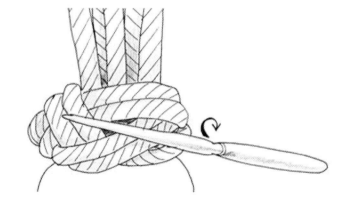

**Standard finish**                    **Footrope finish**

With any luck, your fender will look like one of these two illustrations. If not, you've probably done something wrong. Undo it and start again. Practice makes perfect! Once you've accomplished the fender, all you need is the lanyards to hang them with. See below.

# Attaching your fenders to the vessel

Using a lanyard of similar diameter rope as that used to make your fender, there are two ways to secure your fender to the vessel. The length of the lanyard is determined by how far you want your fender to fall. Then allow an extra 12" [305mm] for tying at each end.

I usually tie one end of my lanyard to the loop in the top of the fender using an anchor hitch (*see page 9*), simply

spliced back to the fall of the rope to make it look tidy. Or you can form an eye splice (*see page 25*) in the end of the lanyard and cow hitch it (*see page 8*) to the loop. Don't be tempted to eye splice straight through the loop as this encourages premature wear on the loop through chafing.

To secure the other end to a suitable rail on the vessel, use a round turn and two half hitches (*see page 20*).

CHAPTER 7

# Covered Fenders

## Buttons
## Tipcats and Barge Fenders
## U-Fenders
## Dwarf's Trousers

Making cores to be covered is a job requiring a great deal of patience, un-tying and re-tying to get the foundation of your fender as firm and solid as possible. You would not build a house on inadequate foundations. You will need additional tools to successfully cut modern car tyres with steel-braced treads.

Making a Dwarf's Trousers core is probably one of the hardest day's work in fender making. Please take extreme care not to catch your fingers, arms, legs or any other part of your anatomy, on protruding tread wire. It hurts, and sometimes goes septic, and bits drop off.

The best way I have found of cutting a tyre that has wire in the tread, is with a 4" [100mm] angle grinder and a 1mm thick stainless steel cutting disk. This leaves very few protruding wires. A finely sharpened, large carving knife is best for cutting the wall of the tyre. An electric jigsaw with a fine wood-cutting blade I have found to be best for cutting out the wired rim. When using power tools, please be careful. Wear protective goggles and gloves.

A final word of warning, don't do your tyre cutting on a Sunday afternoon, you'll upset the neighbours. Burning rubber can be very smelly, and for that reason, do your cutting out of doors and not in a confined space.

# Cores for Buttons for the Stern

You will need tyres with a 4" [100mm] tread, as large a diameter as possible – old fashioned caravan tyres were ideal, being 15" [380mm] plus. Also polypropylene baling twine; a jigsaw with a fine wood-cutting blade is useful for cutting the wall from the tread, being careful not to touch the wires.

If you choose to make a soft button out of cheeses using 2" [50mm] rope, *each cheese* will require approximately 10' [3m]. Obviously if you only have 1" [25mm] rope, twice as much will be needed for each cheese. These suggested lengths are a guide only.

When it comes to buttons for the stern of your vessel, I personally don't like to see anything much over 10" [250mm] long. It is far better to make a tipcat (a type of cushion) on which to sit a smaller-sized button. Longer buttons are difficult to contain and I have seen many boats with their button hanging vertically rather than sitting horizontally, and constantly needing to be put back in position. It is well worth spending a few extra days to make a tipcat first. The results will be far more pleasing and more traditional looking.

When making a core to be covered, never use anything that can rot, i.e. manilla, sizal, hemp, especially if you are covering it with synthetic rope. Cores for buttons can be made in two ways. The method I do NOT recommend is piling several cheeses of rope on top of each other and tying-in using a similar method to that shown on page 75. After a few years, this will tend to lose its shape and look tatty.

My preferred method is to use the treads cut from suitable tyres, which can make a good core for a button. The problem with car tyres is that they are difficult to drill through the wired tread, which is necessary to fix the securing chains in the right place. It is therefore simpler to make the core in two halves.

Supposing you require a 9" [230mm] button, cut two 4" [100mm] car tyre treads and roll each tread as tightly as you can. Once rolled, hold down firmly with your foot or knee to prevent it unrolling. Make a grocer's hitch (*see page 58*) and slip it over the circumference of the rolled car tyre, which you can now elongate and double up to form an approximately 8–9" [200–230mm] circle.

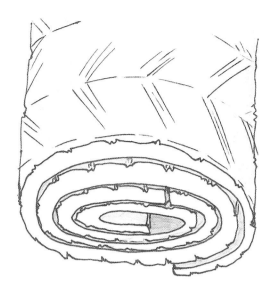

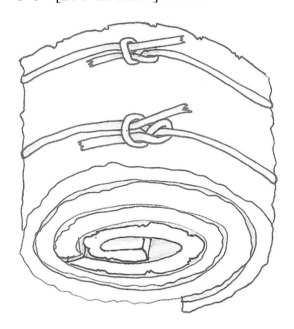

Tighten the grocer's hitch and secure the rolled tread, allowing the coil to open until it measures 7¾ to 8¼" [195–210mm]. Repeat the grocer's hitch so that each side is secured. When you make the second coil, make sure the diameters are identical.

Next we place the chain that will be used to secure the button onto the vessel. I use 4mm long-link chain which is quite sufficient and reasonably strong. At this stage you must decide whether you need two, three or four chains. Should three or four chains be needed, make sure they are shackled firmly together in the centre. Place the chains at the correct exit points and place the second coil firmly on top. I find the button looks better if the finished end of the tread is placed at the bottom of the fender.

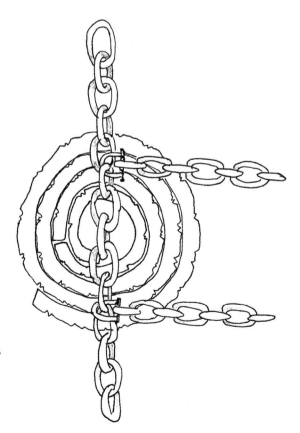

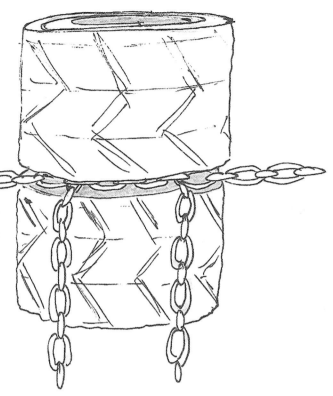

In order to securely join the two coils together, pass your twine through the centre of both coils and, using a grocer's hitch, tie it on the outside, securely trapping the chains and pulling the coils firmly together.

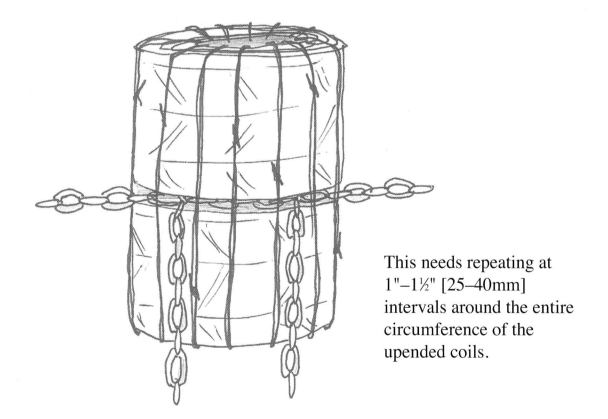

This needs repeating at 1"–1½" [25–40mm] intervals around the entire circumference of the upended coils.

# Cores for Soft Buttons for the Bow

You will need approximately 10' [3m] of 2" [50mm] rope *per cheese*; 3'3" [1m] of 4mm long-link chain for a single chain or 6'6" [2m] for a double; two shackles; cord or baling twine; a carpet needle.

I always make bow buttons of a much larger diameter, usually ending up with an 11" [280mm] core by two layers of 2" [50mm] diameter rope or four layers of 1" [25mm] diameter rope, or as near to that size as possible.

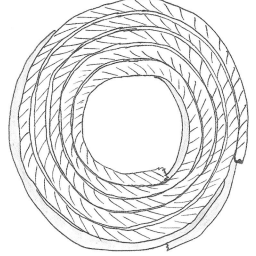

The important thing to remember is to place the chains in position before securely sewing the cheeses together. The entire bundle must be extremely secure, otherwise the button will soon lose its shape and look tatty. Four chains are obviously better for a bow button.

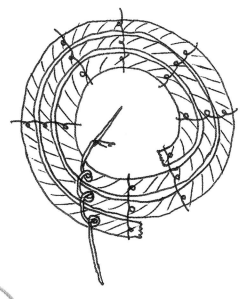

75

# Covering a Button

To start covering a button core,
I use what I call the circular method.
I always start with a 50–65' [16–20m]
length of 12mm-diameter rope, fairly
soft laid if available.

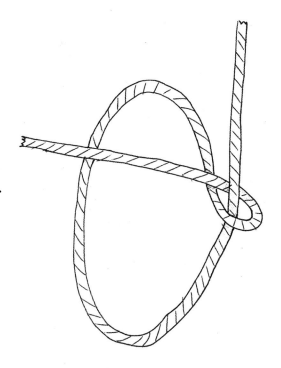

Find the centre and holding it in your left
hand, form a circle using your right hand.
Then pass your right hand over the rope
as it leaves your left hand, and bring to
the front of the loop.

It is important to make sure the loop is
larger than the core you are going to
cover, i.e. if you have a standard 8"
[200mm] core, make sure the loop is at
least 12" [300m].

B

A

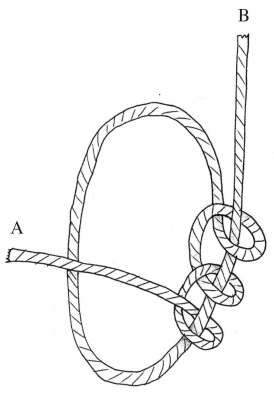

Now all we do is blanket stitch! Otherwise
known as the hitching method. Make sure
you have enough room to place your thumb
side-on between each stitch as it crosses the
main loop. Remember to go over the main
loop *and* the new bight each time. Once
you've worked three to five stitches, place it
over the core to be covered. I usually keep
this very close to, or even touching the
chains, as they exit the core.

If you have tightened the stitches, you will
be able to close the loop fairly snug to your
core, but you should be able to put three or
four fingers between the rope and the core.
It will become tighter as you work.

Make sure the uneven join in the loop is at
what will be the underside of the finished
button, and lock off with a stitch with
standing end B once tightened to the core.
Don't forget to pass your chains through the
loops in order to hold them in position.

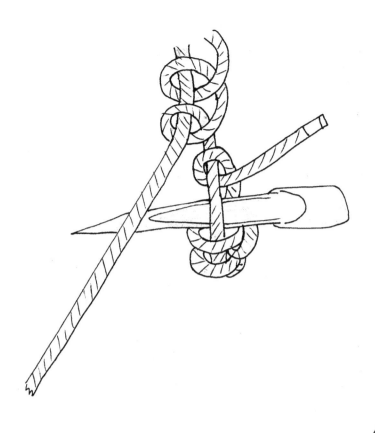

When you have completed the full circle – your first row – for an 8" [200mm] button, you should have approximately 20–22 stitches. Now you can start working using the other fall of the rope, repeating the process, separating each stitch using your Swedish fid.

Once each stitch has been separated by a new stitch, check that you have the same number of stitches on both sides. This can be adjusted by adding an extra stitch through the main loop.

Snug up the stitches as you go, but don't make them too tight.

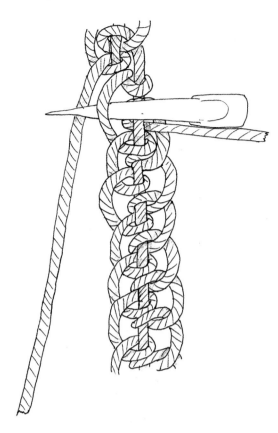

Keep following round. Notice you now have bights to pass through, rather than the original circular loop of rope.

Keep on keeping on until all your rope is finished apart from the last 6–8" [150–200mm].

As you use up your length of rope, a new length is added. I usually add 25–33' [8–10m] at a time.

Instead of passing over, the working end is laid *under* the loop and tight to the core. This could be passed under one of the whippings to hold it securely in position.

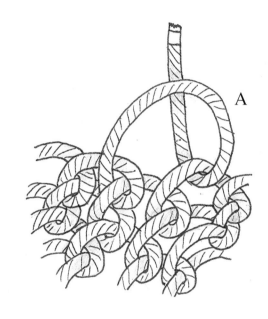

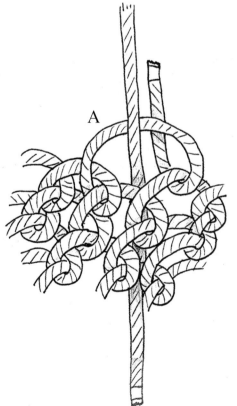

Now pass your new length of rope through loop A and under at least two to four rows of the finished hitching. Your tapered pipe will help here. I usually now hammer a 2–3" [50–75mm] nail through the end of the new strand in order to secure it to the core or other hitches so that a firm stitch can be made without losing the end. When the fender is completely finished, any nails can be removed and the surplus rope cut off tight to the stitches and hidden out of sight.

When you reach the edge of the core, it will be necessary to turn the corner, i.e. close the end. Allow the stitches to stand one stitch higher than the edge, and then gently tap with a soft-faced hammer around the edge in order to set the stitches heading for the centre of the core.

It will of course be necessary to reduce the number of stitches as you work your way towards the centre. I find this could be one stitch in four for the first turn, gradually increasing that ratio in order to decrease the number of stitches. Try to avoid missing a stitch twice in one row, although this is sometimes unavoidable as you get nearer the middle.

As you progress, you may find that your new row of stitches gains on the preceding row, i.e. obscures the earlier stitches, by as much as 75%. This is another good opportunity to miss a stitch. (*See photo page 82*).

Once you have covered the whole, pass the remaining strand underneath the stitches in the direction it wants to travel, and take it to the edge of the button. Repeat with the other side. Cut off any loose material and, using your Swedish fid, hide the ends out of sight.

If you now look at your completed button, you will notice that around its centre there is a row of double stitches. This is quite normal but I always cover these stitches with a Turk's Head. A three-strand, nine-bight Turk's Head is ideal for this purpose.

An 8" x 6" [200mm x 150mm] core will give an approximately 9" x 7" [230mm x 180mm] button. This will take approximately 180' [55m] of rope to cover the button, and 30' [9.5m] of rope for the Turk's Head. Some people choose to use the same colour rope, while others might prefer a contrast.

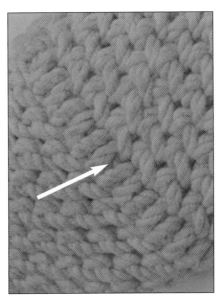

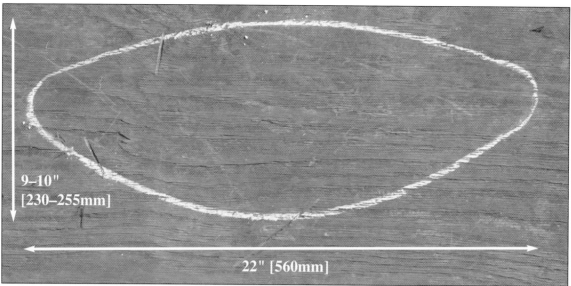

*My chalk outline for a tipcat. These drawings are not to scale!*

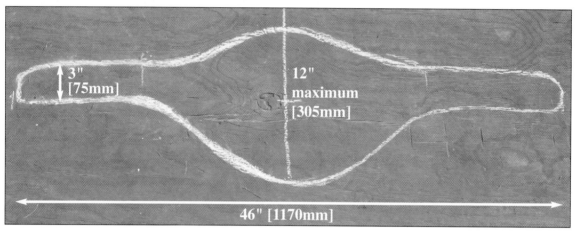

*This outline is the one I use for my barge fenders for narrowboats. You can use poetic license and make your cheeses to any shape you prefer. Barge fenders are built up after making two identical cores to your desired shape but don't forget you will need two centre chains to hang it from either side of the stem (or bow). Additional cheeses need to be added to 'pudding out' the centre of your barge fender, tapering equally to both ends. It should have a girth of around 30" [760mm].*

*This is the core for Big Bertha, an extra-large barge fender for a Dutch barge. Notice the graduated layers of rope which dictate the size and shape.*

# Cores and Covers
# for Barge Fenders and Tipcats

For a tipcat core, you will need 9'9" [3m] of 2" [50mm] diameter rope; polypropylene baling twine or 3mm-diameter cord; 1 meter of 4mm long-link chain; carpet needle. The best method of starting the tipcat core, which will be made of rope, would be to draw on the floor of your workshop, the shape that suits your taste. Measure the outside line carefully with a flexible tape – I use a tailor's cloth tape measure. I find 22" [560mm] is a good length for a standard tipcat, and 9–10" [230–255mm] for the width. When covered, it will increase to 24" [610mm] long and 11–12" [280–305mm] wide. Join the two ends of the outer rope together with a butt joint. This can be achieved by heating synthetic rope to melting point, and pressing firmly together. Now hold the outer rope to your desired shape, and firmly pack the inside using mis-shaped cheese, rope oddments, etc.

You will need to make two of the following, and it is important that they are exactly the same size. Cut a length of the thickest rope you can find, 2" [50mm] will be best. Place it around the outline of the shape you have drawn on the floor, then cut more individual pieces of rope to coil tightly inside it.

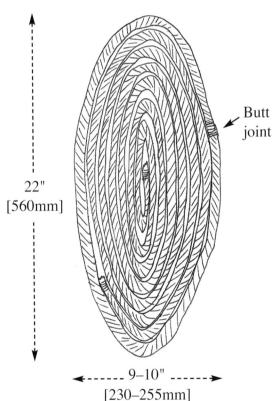

Butt joint

22" [560mm]

9–10" [230–255mm]

Once the entire area is filled as tightly as possible, sew each piece of rope in place. A large, curved carpet needle is absolutely ideal for this purpose. Next carefully turn it over and sew it again on the other side.

If you have no choice but to use a smaller diameter rope, you must make additional cheeses to give a minimum core thickness of 4" [100mm]. When covered, this will increase to about 5" [125mm]. You may want to increase this to 6" [150mm] which again, when covered, will increase to approximately 7" [180mm]. If so, you will need to make three cheeses of 2" [50mm] rope.

It is a lot more difficult to get a firm tipcat core if you are making it with more layers. For the purposes of this book, I shall assume we are working with two 2" [50mm] cheeses, which is the ideal.

Once you have made your identical cores, you are ready to make a chain sandwich. Place the chain across the centre of the first cheese, with several links spare at each side, say 6–8" [150–200mm].

Secure the chain in place by overstitching with your carpet needle and twine. Now place the second identical cheese on top, and secure together using grocer's hitches.

I always cover my tipcat fenders using the hitching method (blanket stitch) *(see page 76)*. Remember to start in the middle at its widest point and every time the covering starts to get baggy, i.e. you can put more than three fingers between the covering and the core, this is an indication that you need to drop a stitch. To do this, simply miss one loop.

As you progress, you may find that your new row of stitches gains on the preceding row, i.e. obscures the earlier stitches, by as much as 75%, as shown here. This is another good opportunity to miss a stitch.

# Cores for Dwarf's Trousers

You will need two 14" [360mm] tyres, conventional not low profile, one with a 4–5" [100–125mm] tread width, which will be cut in half. The first half will be used for the body and legs of the dwarf's trousers, and the second half tread only will be used as the centre coil. The second tyre should have a tread width of 5½–6" [140–152mm] and the tread only will be used as a final wrap. When visiting your tyre fitter, select well-worn tyres with minimal tread left, if any.

You will also need approximately 8' [2.5m] of 4mm long-link chain or similar; two D-shackles; 2–3mm cord or polypropylene baling twine, which makes a cheaper substitute; 6'6"–9' [2–2.75m] of 4mm long-link chain. Useful additional tools – drill, 1" [25mm] hole saw (metal cutting); 4–4½" [100–115mm] angle grinder with 1mm stainless steel cutting disk; jigsaw with a fine wood-cutting blade; a finely sharpened large knife.

I find that a 14" [360mm] car tyre with a 4–5" [100–125mm] wide tread is ideal for Dwarf's Trousers. Cut the tyre in half, having first removed the steel edging, i.e. the rim that fits on the wheel. A jigsaw is ideal for this purpose.

Next trim along the dotted line using a jigsaw or sharp knife. Trim the soft wall from as tight to the wire in the tread as possible, extending some 8" [200mm] back from the ends.

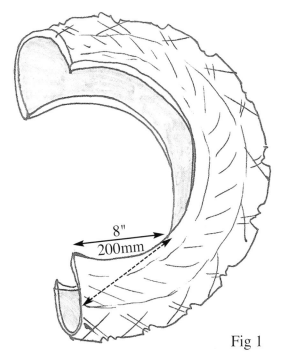

8"
200mm

Fig 1

Find the centre and drill a hole in the centre of the tread (hole A). This needs to be something in the order of ¾" [20mm]. It is sometimes difficult, but a hole saw or a hole punch can be used. Depending on the construction of tread wires, it is sometimes possible to drill a hole with a steel bit.

Then 4" [100mm] either side of that central hole, drill further holes of the same size (holes B and C), and two more holes at each end of the half tyre (holes D and E), five holes in total. This is a smelly process and best done outdoors.

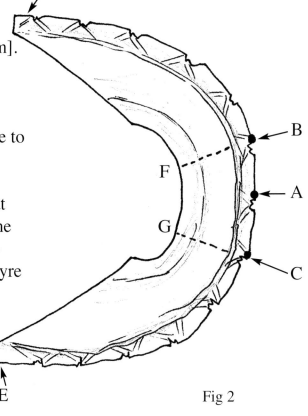

Fig 2

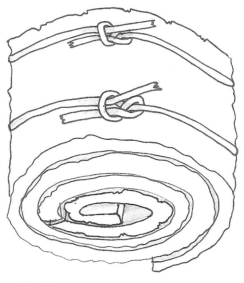

Fig 3

Now cut the tread off another tyre, 4½–5" [115–125mm] is the ideal tread width, and roll it very tightly as described for the button core (*see page 73*), but do not allow it to be more than 6" [150mm] in diameter. Secure as previously described under button cores.

To decide the length of your main chain, using your soft tape, measure the circumference of your half-tyre, and add an extra 16" [410mm], in order to allow 6–8" [150–200mm] to protrude from each end. Two further chains need to be cut, approximately 12" [305mm] or longer.

To fix it in place, thread a piece of cord approximately 24" [610mm] long, through hole B from the outside to the inside, and through a link of chain that has been correctly positioned. Don't forget to leave an equal amount of chain protruding from each end.

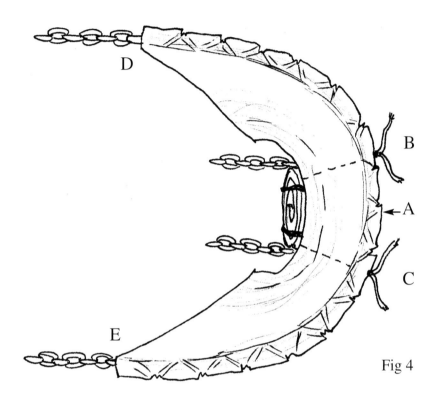

Fig 4

Then bring the cord out of hole A to the outside of the tyre once again trapping an appropriate link, back in through hole C and then back out through hole A. Tie the two ends of the cord together as tightly as possible. Once again, a grocer's hitch is ideal.

Now cut two more pieces of cord approximately 18–20" [460–510mm] long. Pass 6" [150mm] of each cord through the two remaining holes at each end of the tread, D and E, from the outside to the inside. Pass through

a convenient link of chain and temporarily tie the ends together. A bow as in tying shoelaces is ideal for this, but remember one end will be longer than the other.

Cut two more lengths of cord approximately 24" [610mm] long. Centre the coiled tyre tread inside the half tyre over hole A, and using one piece of cord for holes A and B, and the second piece of cord for holes A and C, securely tie as tightly as possible, trapping the chain in position.

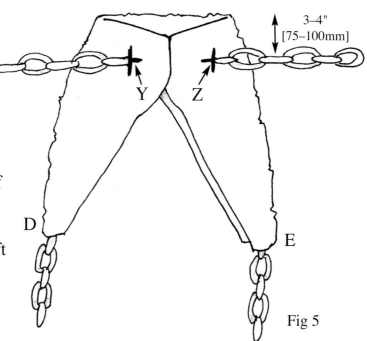

Approximately 3" [75mm] either side of the edge of the coil, shackle a short length of chain – 16" [400mm] will be plenty – to the main chain on each side. Now bend the sides of the tyre to form the shape shown in Fig 5. Cut two crosses [Y and Z] in the soft side wall to allow the shackled chains to pass through and out of the top.

3–4"
[75–100mm]

Y    Z

D

E

Fig 5

Now place a grocer's hitch as a whipping below the chains, as in Fig. 6. Make a cut half way through the soft wall of the tyre, as in L and M. This needs repeating both back and front.

Now untie the temporary shoe-lace bows at D and E and make final adjustments to the tension of the chains. Take the 6" [150mm] end of cord that is on the inside of the tyre, pass it through the nearest link, and pass it back out of the same hole (D or E). Now force the tyre to form as near to a circle as possible, making sure the finished diameter is the same on both sides, and trapping the chains as tightly as you can. This can be difficult but not impossible. Using the remaining longer length of the cord, tighten securely with as many turns as the cord allows – at least three – and still be able to tighten using the grocer's hitch.

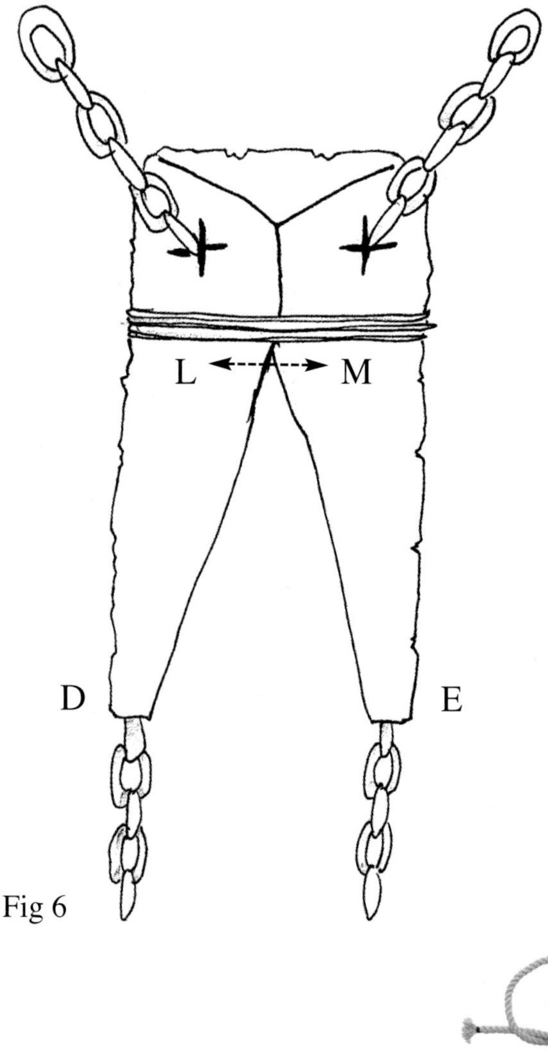

L ◄--┼--► M

D

E

Fig 6

At this point, I stuff the legs with short ends of scrap rope. The cut walls of the tyre (inside leg) need to be almost closed together so beware of making it too fat. You simply want to make a nice-shaped leg throughout its length, from chain to inner coiled tyre. It is necessary to cut the tyre wall half way towards the tread from the centre to enable a pleasing shape at the crotch end of the core. See L and M on Fig. 6.

Now tie firm whippings every two inches using grocer's hitches, working up from the whippings where the chains are tied at holes D and E.

Fig 7

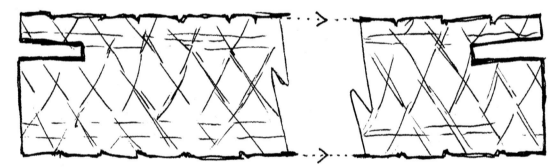

Fig 8

To finish the dwarf's trousers core, take the tyre with the tread width of around 5½" [140mm]. Carefully measure the circumference of what will be the nose of the fender (the

dwarf's waistband), then cut a piece of tread to that exact length, plus 2" [50mm]. Make two slits in the tyre (*as seen in Fig 8*), 3" [75mm] from the front edge.

Position one slit over one chain, and wrap the tyre tread securely around until the second slit will go over the second chain. Again fasten securely. This will overlap slightly between chains, do not worry, as this will make the fender look more rounded. Securely bind with twine using further grocer's hitches. If it is not quite a perfect round, any gaps can be packed out by forcing small sections of the remaining unused tyre tread beneath this final layer.

Fig 9

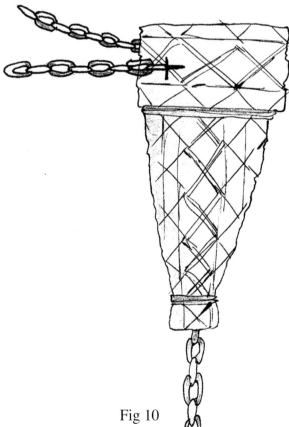

Fig 10

Your Dwarf's Trousers core should resemble Fig 10.

Before starting to cover the Dwarf's Trousers, check and double check that both legs are the same size and length.

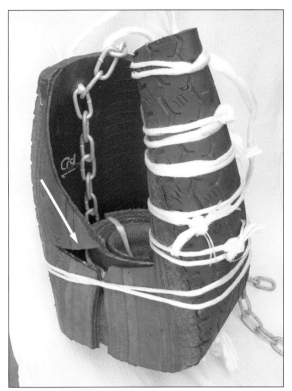

*The underside of the fender, showing the cut half-way through the wall of the tyre and the coil in place, inside the tummy.*

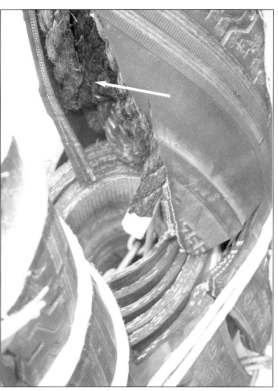

*Note how the inside of each leg is packed tight with short ends of spare rope before lashing into shape.*

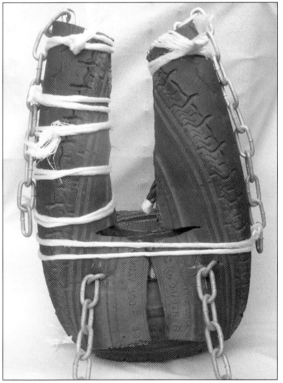

*This shows both cuts to the tyre wall.*

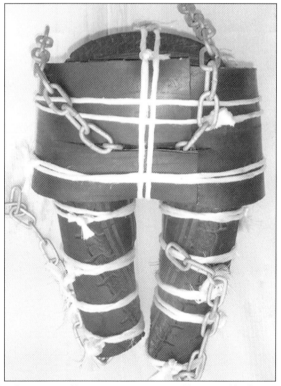

*The Dwarf's Trousers core all parcelled up and ready to cover.*

# Covering Dwarf's Trousers

If you have already made a button, (*see page 76*), you will know how to start and how to close the front of a pair of dwarf's trousers. But this time, starting with 50–65' [15–20m] of rope, instead of losing the end of your rope and cutting off, we bring it through to either the top or the bottom of the fender. You will have had to a new length of rope; it doesn't matter how much rope is left, in fact the longer the better. So you will have two working ends before starting the crotch of the trousers.

The picture on the right shows the working end from the front, when to stop covering the main button and when to cross the crotch and start the right leg. Make sure your first stitch for the first leg is exactly half-way round so that you have the same amount of stitches around each leg.

Here it's time to add a new length of rope. Take the strand that you have used to cover the fender so far, and stitch away until it too reaches the appropriate place to bring through the crotch.

It will soon become obvious how and when to cover these two inside strands in similar fashion to that of starting.

Now work each leg alternately, one row of stitches on one leg, then a row on the other leg, to make sure that you have the same amount of stitches and rows, and that they are decreased equally. I find it best policy to try and drop stitches either on the inside of the leg, or on what will be the underside of the fender.

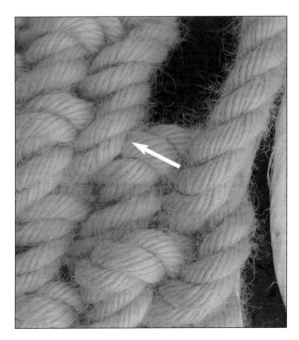

On the right here, you can see that it is just about time to drop a stitch. Failure to drop stitches as it becomes necessary, causes the stitches to bunch up and are difficult to hammer down to make it look attractive.

Using your tapered pipe, you can add
a strand by entering at point A,
exiting at point B, and passing the
new rope through both the loop and
previous stitches before removing the
pipe. I often pin the end of the new
rope with a nail, temporarily securing
it to prevent it being pulled through
as more stitches are worked.

Once again using your tapered pipe,
enter at A, coming out as close as
you can to your last stitch, pass your
unused rope through the pipe,
remove pipe and tighten any slack.
Tapping with a hammer as you pull
should make a nice neat finish.

This picture shows the loop through
which we can add another length of
rope. (*See page 78 for a drawing of
this step.*)

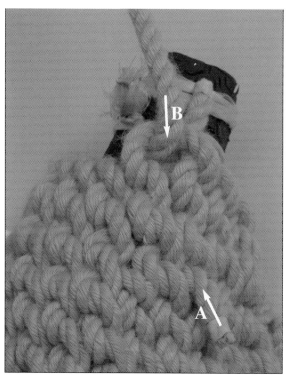

When you get to the very tip of the
leg, you will find you have to reduce
stitches rapidly. Make sure your
stitches rest snugly on the chain.

# U Fender – Core and Covering

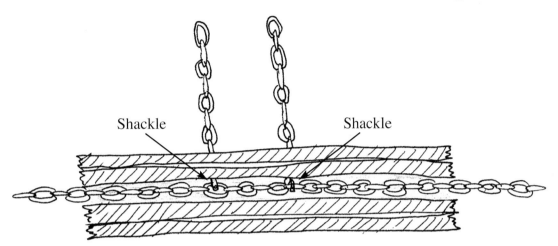

Shackle          Shackle

One of the simplest covered fenders to make is the U fender. This is usually draped around the bow of your narrowboat, sometimes below a Dwarf's Trousers, to give some protection against the low-lying sill in a lock. I am sure by this stage in the book, these simple drawings will teach you all there is to know about making a U fender core.

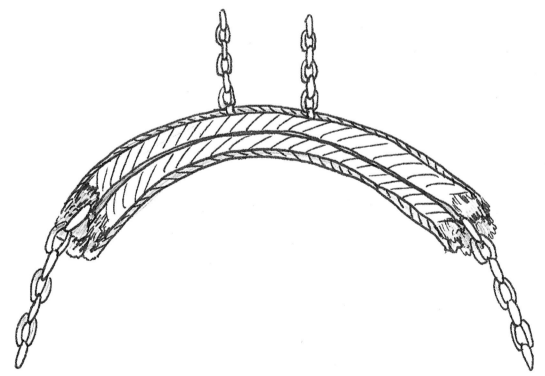

The core needs to end up measuring about 34" [865mm] long to make a 36" [900mm] covered fender, and needs to be 3–4" [75–100mm] in diameter. I usually crown this fender and finish by placing a Five Three Turk's Head between the top chains to give it a finished look.

The main difficulty with the U fender is having to accurately calculate how much rope we need. It must be enough to complete the fender, because it is difficult to join in extra lengths.

One way of calculating the length needed for 12mm-diameter rope, is based on the fact that one stitch takes approximately 4" [100mm] of rope to cover a distance of 1" [25mm], a factor of 4. So if your fender core is 34" [865mm], you will need approximately

> 34" x 4 = 136" or 11'4"
> [865 x 4 = 3.46m]

of rope but I would add a good 20% to be safe; this totals 13'6" [4.15m].

Now measure the circumference of your core. Let's say it is 10" [250mm].

You can now see this makes a ½" [12.5mm] of rope and a ½" [12.5mm] gap between each strand, which are then lashed or whipped around the core.

You will therefore need 10 strands measuring 13'6" [4.15m] long.

*Tip*: Place a masking tape marker exactly half-way along each strand of rope. It helps when centring the rope on the fender core and you can see if any of the strands move whilst tightening your first couple of rows when crowning.

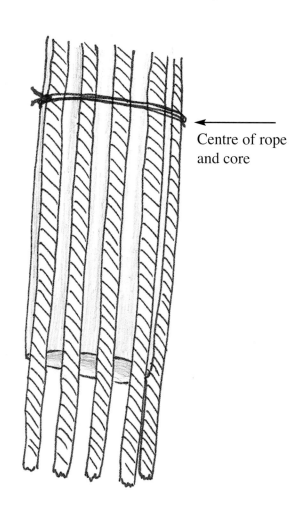

Centre of rope and core

You should find covering the U fender fairly easy, because you are already well-practiced at crowning, since that was how we made the bottle fender (*see pages 28 and 61*).

Start crowning from the whipping. Once you've worked to the end in one direction, remove the whipping and tighten any slack before working the other side. Don't forget to change direction on each completed circuit.

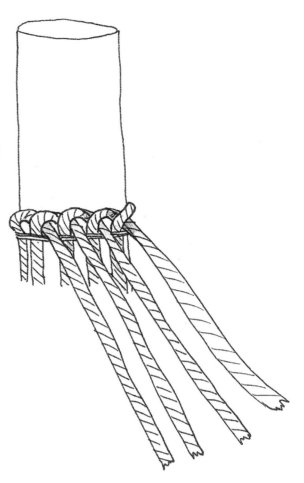

When you have reached the end, you can either hide the strands back up inside the fender – see the Standard Finish for the bottle fender, (*see page 66*). Or if your surplus rope is long enough, using only four strands, you could complete your U fender with the Footrope Knot finish used for the bottle fender, (*see page 67*). The surplus strands can then be cut off to reveal a fluffy collar around the end chains.

Your finished U fender will be fairly flexible and you should be able to bend it quite easily to the shape you require.

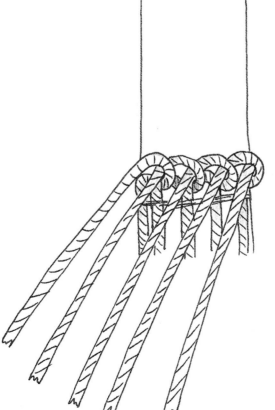

# CHAPTER 8

# Fancy Ropework

Fancy ropework has always had a purpose, it was never purely for decoration. The best example of this is probably the rope safety ladder. for which there was a definite and obvious need. It was probably only because the owners had time during the long dark evenings to embellish their handiwork, that even the most utilitarian items became decorative too.

Cabin strings also arose from necessity. Even horse- and boat-owners employed by a cargo company had to supply their own tow ropes, so it made sense to look after them carefully. (*See page 109*).

I have included Donut Fenders in this section because they are very impractical in use and offer little protection, but look extremely attractive. And as you will have mastered the Lanyard Knot once you've made the rope safety ladder, you will be well equipped to tackle this project too.

As with all fancy ropework, it was also a way of showing off your skills. Tingle Buttons in either spider weave or basket weave can look quite charming, but they had a definite purpose.

On a butty, the rudder is held together just above the water-line with two pieces of wood called tingles. A small button about 6" [150mm] across and no more than 4" [100mm] thick, would be secured to the tingles in order to prevent damage, water entry and rotting to the end-grain of the timber.

Spider weave or basket weave can of course be used on larger fenders in thicker rope than would be used for the Tingle Button.

# Rope Safety Ladder

I t's occurred to most of us at one time or another. If you have the misfortune to fall in, how the heck do you get back OUT? So as well as being fun and satisfying to make for yourself, and even ornamental, the addition of a rope ladder will make your vessel a lot safer too. I was at sea for the best part of 40 years and did not fall in once. Yet within a year of owning a narrowboat, I had fallen in twice! I very soon made myself a rope ladder and this is how I did it.

Once it's made, suspend it by the top loop from a T-bar, dolly or cleat, and tie it up out of the water using cotton, but obviously within reach of anyone in the water below. This will keep it high enough and dry, but the cotton is easily broken in an emergency. Remember, polypropylene will float, so the ladder will have to be pulled under the water to allow you to get your foot on the lowest tread.

Making this ladder will teach you the Lanyard Knot, the Matthew Walker Knot and to practise again the Footrope Knot.

Estimating the length of 12mm rope you need for this project is important because you cannot have any joins. It seems to take miles and miles but for a 2-rung rope ladder, allow 33' [10m] a 4-rung rope ladder, allow 39' [12m].

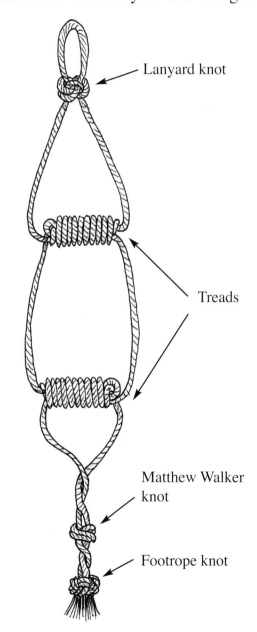

Lanyard knot

Treads

Matthew Walker knot

Footrope knot

# The Lanyard Knot - also known as the Diamond Knot

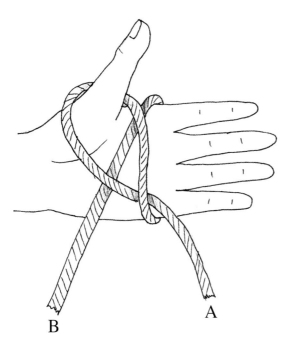

Find the centre of the rope, i.e. the half way point, and place a piece of masking tape around the rope to mark this spot. Holding the masking tape in your left hand, take it over the palm and allow the rope to drop both sides. Make a bight in the fall from behind your hand, using your thumb as a measure.

Remove the bight from your thumb, and place it over the rope across your palm, holding the top of the loop with your thumb.

Taking strand B, which is furthest to the left of your work, pass it under strand A and lock off the ladder in the palm of your hand.

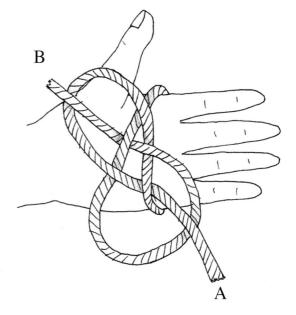

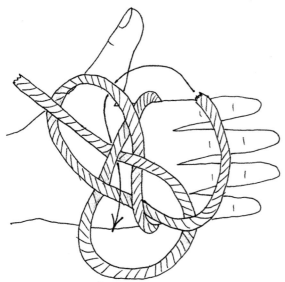

Continuing with strand A, pass the working end over the loop around your hand, under everything by your upturned thumb, and bring it out through the centre of the knot, which will have four sides. If you cannot count four sides, it is not the right place.

Now using working end B, pass it under everything except the strand that goes round your hand. This also emerges from the four-sided centre of the knot.

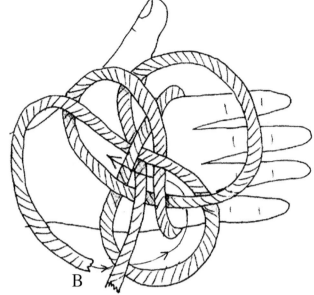

Remove all slack, once again being careful not to remove too much at a time. Using your pointed-nose pliers, work it through gently. You may find the loop can be extended as you work. Work it back through the loop into the knot until it reaches one of the falls and the loop is no longer than 6"[150mm]. I think 4" [100mm] is probably better.

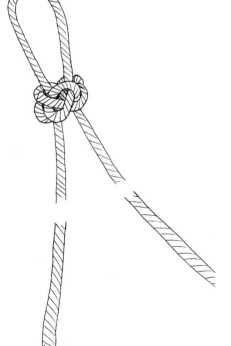

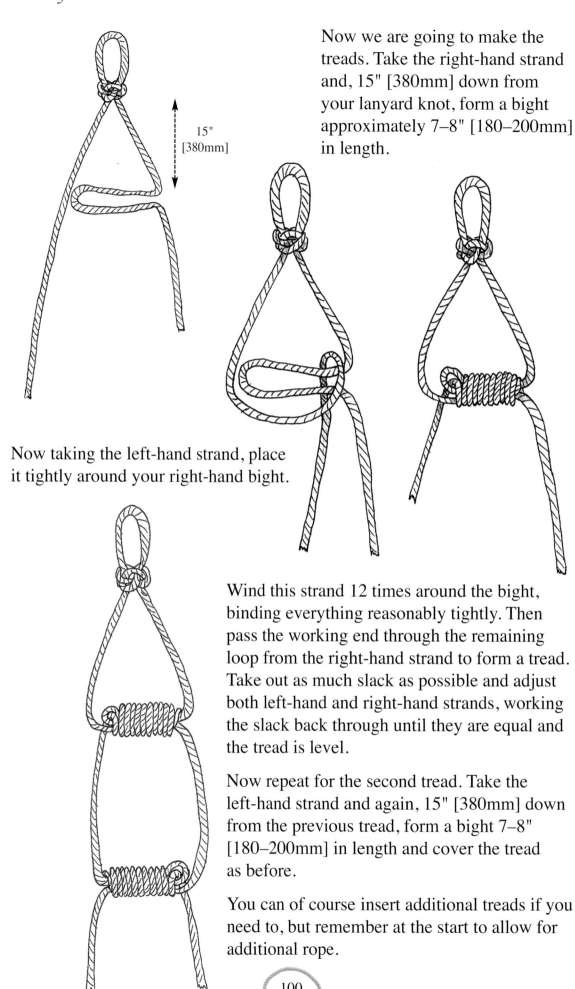

Now we are going to make the treads. Take the right-hand strand and, 15" [380mm] down from your lanyard knot, form a bight approximately 7–8" [180–200mm] in length.

Now taking the left-hand strand, place it tightly around your right-hand bight.

Wind this strand 12 times around the bight, binding everything reasonably tightly. Then pass the working end through the remaining loop from the right-hand strand to form a tread. Take out as much slack as possible and adjust both left-hand and right-hand strands, working the slack back through until they are equal and the tread is level.

Now repeat for the second tread. Take the left-hand strand and again, 15" [380mm] down from the previous tread, form a bight 7–8" [180–200mm] in length and cover the tread as before.

You can of course insert additional treads if you need to, but remember at the start to allow for additional rope.

# The Matthew Walker Knot

Of the two strands, take the right-hand strand and make a bight about 12" [300mm] down from the bottom of the last tread.

Form an ordinary overhand knot.

Now form another bight, this time using the left-hand strand as it leaves the ladder on the top of the existing overhand knot previously tied.

Now pass the end through the back and through both loops.

After removing all slack, and with a little bit of jiggery pokery, it should look like this. Don't get disheartened if it doesn't work first time. Even now, after all these years, I sometimes have to tie and re-tie a couple of times to get it to look right.

Later in this book I will be asking you to tie 6- and 8-strand Matthew Walker knots, so the more practice you get at this stage, the better you will do then.

I think at this stage it is nice to put a twist in the ropes. This can be achieved by holding both strands in one hand, about 6" 150mm] down from your successfully completed Matthew Walker knot. Taking the top strand, twist it anti-clockwise, i.e. to tighten the lay. Pull it over the strand beneath and apply pressure with your thumb, and take what is now the top strand. Repeat the twisting, then bring it over the top and down the front of the other strand, making that one the bottom stand.

Now tie a constrictor knot pretty near your thumb. Separate the lay of both ropes, which will give you six strands. Don't forget to whip the ends with masking tape to prevent unravelling. (By this stage of the book, you should not need telling!)

Next tie a footrope knot which you have done before on the bottle fender (*see page 67*).

Cut off the strands about 1½" [40mm] below the footrope knot, and unlay all the fibres in order to form a nice bushy tassel. A dog's brush is ideal for teasing out.

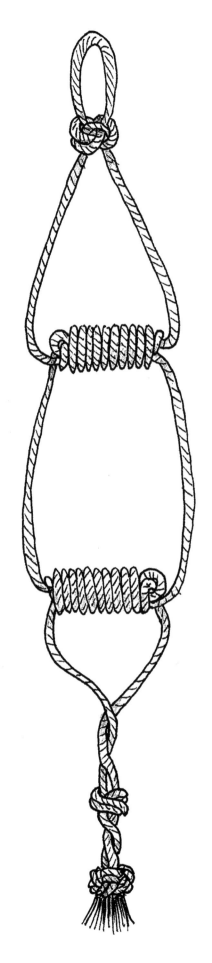

103

# The Legend of the Matthew Walker Knot

*L*egend has it that Matthew Walker was the Master of a privateer vessel (closely akin to a pirate ship) in the 1780s. He was captured off the Asian coast, imprisoned and sentenced to death.

Whilst awaiting execution, he was befriended by the Emperor, who was apparently a keen knot tyer himself. They spent many hours together in Walker's cell, enjoying their mutual passion for knots.

One day, Matthew Walker told the Emperor he could tie a knot in a piece of rope that was impossible to untie without destroying the rope. The Emperor immediately threw down the challenge that if he could do such a thing, he would be granted a free Pardon.

Whereupon, Matthew Walker requested 7 fathoms of 3-strand rope (a fathom equals 6 feet), unlaid the rope half way along its length, and tied his knot. He relaid the rope, neatly whipping each end, and presented it to the Emperor.

Despite considerable thought and effort, the Emperor could not untie the knot and Matthew Walker was granted his Pardon. The knot has been named after him ever since.

It was used on the old sea-going square-rigged ships as a terminal knot or stopper knot to hold the lower end of the main rigging. The lanyards (as these ropes are called) were passed through a banded piece of hard wood strapped to the hull, and held fast by this bulky yet decorative knot. You can imagine the results if it had slipped or given way!

# Donut Fenders

First take 40' [12m] of 12mm rope, polypropylene is perfectly adequate for these fenders. Form a tight cheese with an outside diameter of 12" [300mm] and a hole in the centre measuring 4" [100mm]. It should ideally be approximately 2½" [65mm] thick. Now hold it *loosely* in shape with whippings.

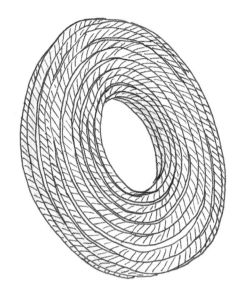

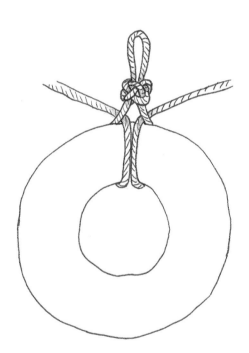

Now take a 30' [9.5m] length of rope, mark the middle with masking tape and tie a Lanyard Knot (*see page 98*). This is then cow-hitched snug but not too tightly around the cheese. The cheese will probably pull out of shape at this stage, and may take some persuading to keep its desired shape.

Bring the working end over the front of the work and through the bight it has created.

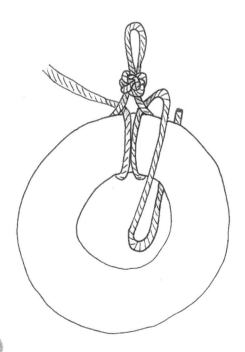

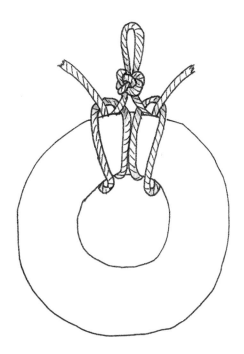

Repeat with the other working strand and continue in the same fashion. Also continue re-shaping the fender as it will try to distort with each hitch you make.

Keep on keeping on in the same style until each side meets at the bottom of the donut.

The edge of your finished fender should look like this. Now you can remove the loose whippings. You will be able to take any remaining rope left over from your hitches and circle it round within the hitches in order to lose the ends. This will also make it just a little bit firmer.

# Tingle Button

The core for the Tingle Button is merely a coil of rope. How much you need depends on the size you are planning to make. This one is 6" [150mm]. It helps to coil it around a suitably-sized round object. In the past I have used old-fashioned milk bottles or even a log from the fireplace.

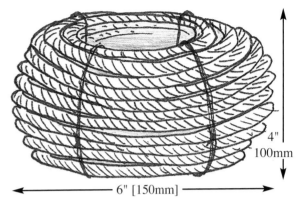

Don't forget to add your chains through the coils of rope. A smaller chain is better for this size of fender.

To cover you will need 33' [10m] of 6mm rope; more may be added later, but first take a separate piece of the same rope to make the framework on which you will weave.

Pull the working end of your rope through the centre hole of the coiled core for a length of some 6'6" [2m], depending on the thickness of the rope you are using. Tingle buttons were traditionally done with a finer rope, say 6–8mm diameter, but should you choose to cover a larger fender in this way, then once again 12mm rope would be OK, but remember to adjust the length accordingly.

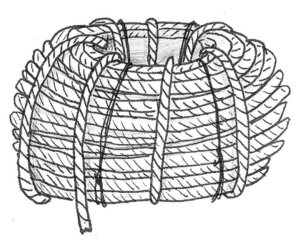

Wrap your working end continually over and around the coiled core, from the inside to the outside, *as shown*. It must be loose enough to place two or three fingers between these strands and the core. It will tighten significantly as you work. When you have worked your way round and are back to where you started, join the shorter ends to the longer working end with a whipping that isn't too bulky. This forms your framework on which to weave, and you can continue with the longer working end.

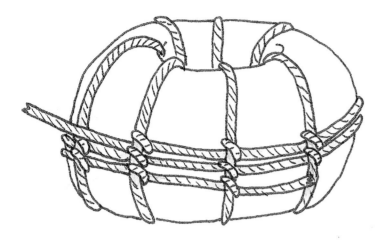

## Spider Weave

To cover your Tingle Button using spider weave, start from the inside and pass the working end under each strand of the framework, over the top and back under, ready for the next. Continue in this fashion all the way round, both inside and outside.

I have shown this on the outside for clarity but you will obviously need to start inside the centre and work outwards. Keep each row as tight as possible to its predecessor.

New lengths can be added by hiding the finished end under the completed work. The new end should also be hidden, but from the opposite direction.

## Basket Weave

If you prefer, you can use a basket weave covering. For this your framework ropes must be an odd number, 5, 7 or 9, according to the desired size of your fender. Then, simply starting from the inside of your core, go over one strand and under the next until your fender is covered. Keep the rows as tightly together as possible.

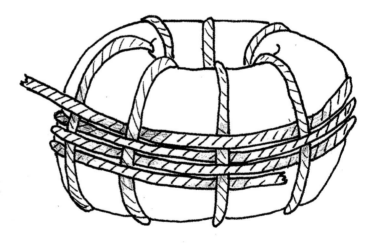

# Cabin Strings

Cabin strings were originally used on horse-drawn boats when their 110-foot tow-lines were wet or damp after a day's work. Once the wet ropes had been carefully coiled, the centre cabin string would be wrapped through and around the coil, and the dolly would hold the coiled rope away from the cabin side.

The other two dollies hang either side of the centre string, and would have been placed at approximately '20 minutes to' and '20 minutes past' in order to hold the coil of rope and allow air to pass freely around it.

This would then be hung near the chimney in the boatman's cabin so that the wet rope could dry out, avoiding the risk of allowing it to rot. (*See colour photo page 115*).

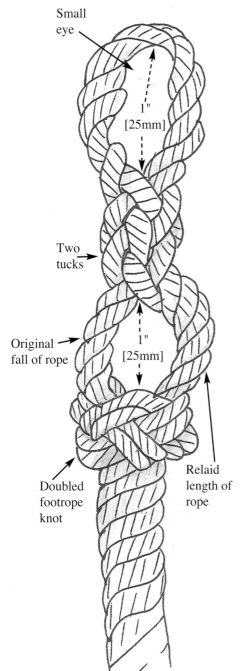

Small eye

1"
[25mm]

Two tucks

Original fall of rope

1"
[25mm]

Doubled footrope knot

Relaid length of rope

## The Centre String

We start by making the shorter centre string. Take a 6'6" [2m] length of 12mm bleached or unbleached Egyptian cotton rope. Unlay the rope for about 15" [380mm] and put a masking tape whipping at the end of each strand to prevent it unravelling.

Now splice a small eye using only two tucks, instead of the customary four. Arrange the three unlaid strands together, away from the main fall of the rope, and re-lay as tightly as possible and as near to the original lay of the rope as you can manage. To do this, take the top strand of unlaid rope, twist it clockwise as you bring it down over the front of the second and third strands to become the bottom strand, holding it in place with your thumb. Continue taking the top strand, twisting it clockwise and bringing it across to the bottom. This will give you a parallel run of rope, 1½–2" [40–50mm] will be sufficient.

Then splice it back to the main fall of the rope for one tuck. Using the remaining length of the unlaid strands, either form a doubled footrope knot (*see page 67*), or if you prefer, cover the splicing tuck with a Five Four Turk's Head made in 3–4mm cotton line.

Tighten it up until hard. To do this, pull up the slack with your pointed-nose pliers just a small portion at a time to ensure that the footrope knot tightens equally. If you take too much at a time, you may find it becomes irretrievably lopsided.

Once all slack has been removed, and you are happy with the symmetry of the finished footrope knot, cut off any surplus material as tightly as possible, taking care not to damage either the footrope knot or the main rope.

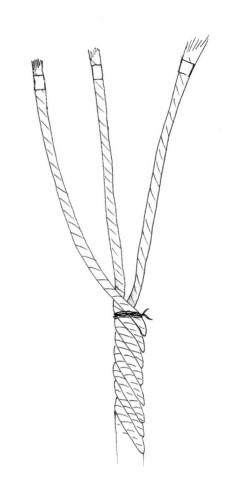

## Crowning the Dolly

We are now going to make the dolly at the other end of the rope.

Place a temporary whipping 29–30" [740–760mm] down from the top of the loop. You should now have 3' [915mm] left to unlay and form a crown, as if starting a back splice (*see page 28*).

At this point, it is best to hang your work from an overhead hook by the first eye splice you made. Unlike when making a fender, you are now only using three strands and all crowns will be heading in an anti-clockwise direction when looking at it with the first crown at the bottom.

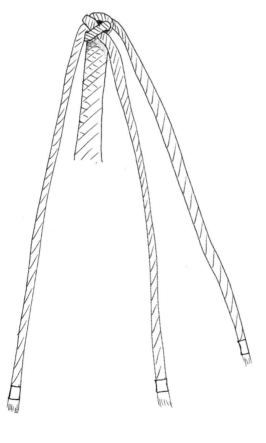

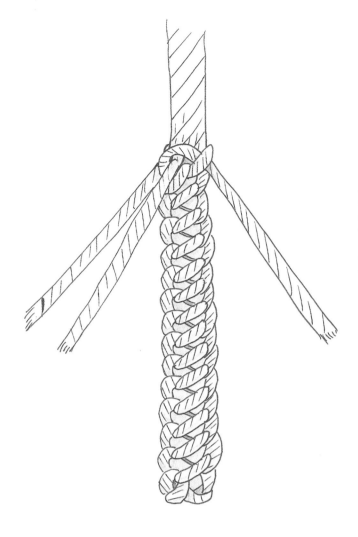

Repeat the crowning procedure 14 times more. This should give your dolly a body length of 6" [150mm].

Splice through the main rope using one set of tucks. Then form another doubled footrope knot on top to finish the body.

Remove all slack and cut off spare strands as tight to the knot as possible, being careful not to damage the footrope knot or the main rope.

# The Second String

For the second string, you will need a longer length of rope 9'6" [2.9m]. Put a temporary constrictor knot whipping 36" [915mm] from one end and repeat the earlier instructions for making the dolly, ensuring that the length is exactly the same (14 crowns).

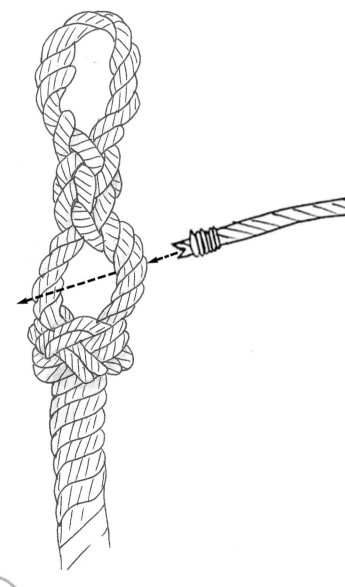

Now pass the unworked end of this second string through the lower of the two eye splices of the centre string you made earlier.

113

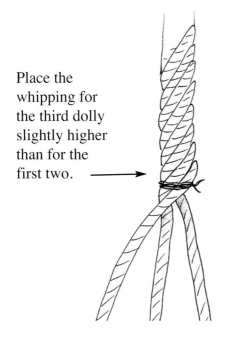

Place the whipping for the third dolly slightly higher than for the first two. ———→

Now line up the bottom of the two dollies and on the third string, place a whipping slightly higher than on the previous two – approximately ¼–⅜" [6–8mm] up from the crown. As before, unlay the rope, again using masking tape to prevent unravelling.

Once again, crown and check that all three dollies are now level. Some adjustment may be needed. Remove the whipping and proceed as described previously.

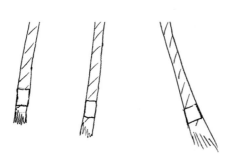

## Single-strand Cabin String

Should you want just a single cabin string, you need make only one splice, leaving out the re-laid rope section of the 3-strand cabin string.

The length can of course be varied to suit your purpose.

*Cabin strings on the side of Knot Krazy.*

This final chapter continues into the colour plate section because some of the more complicated knots, such as the Star Knot, and the more decorative pieces such as the tiller tassel, are better shown in colour.

115

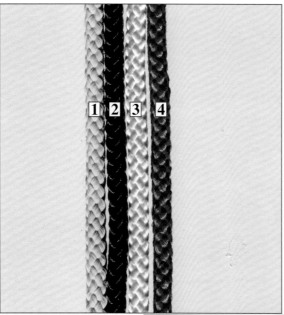

# The French Senate

We are now going to make a French senate, which can be used for forming the top loop of keyrings, tiller tassels, etc., or for a section of the body if made using 8 strands. Arrange the strands coming from the whipping flat across the first and second fingers and thumb of your left hand. Counting from left to right, mentally number them 1 to 4.

Take strand 1, pass it behind strands 2 and 3, and bring it back over the front of strand 3 to become the new strand 2. Take strand 4 behind strands 3 and 2 and back to form the new strand 3.

Take strand 1, pass behind 2 and 3 and back to form the new strand 2.

Repeat the sequence until you reach the desired length. Practise this a few times until you can get it neat and tight before committing to an actual project.

Once you've doubled this to form a top loop, you will have eight strands, ideal for an 8-strand Matthew Walker knot (*see page 118 for the 6-strand version*). Or, with just 4 or 6 of the strands, you could choose to make a footrope knot.

## The Doubled French Senate

Now try the same thing with doubled strands, and it should look like this.

117

# Keyrings and Tiller Tassels

Keyrings have an obvious purpose, and knot tyers the world over have had fun creating their own designs. And now you can too.

Even the apparently ornamental tiller tassel has a purpose: better to feel that tickling the back of your neck as you stand up from releasing the mooring line, than to bang your head on the tiller pin!

We have already learned most of the knots we will need for these items, but let's also master the Matthew Walker Knot and the Star Knot first.

## The Matthew Walker Knot

You have already had experience of a two-strand Matthew Walker knot, when we made the rope ladder (*see page 101*). This is a 6-strand knot, but it can be made with any number of strands. Arrange all your strands in a straight line but if this is not possible because they come from a senate, start with the top strand and work in a clockwise direction.

Starting here the green strand, form an overhand knot trapping the remaining five strands. Put another way, make a green loop over the top of your work and then bring the green working end behind the other stands and bring it out of its own loop. With the next strand, which here will be the white one, do the same but go through the green loop as well as the white loop.

Continue the same procedure with all other colours, making sure you go through all the loops.

Now comes the fiddly bit. Remove as much slack as is necessary to start to try and make some sense of what you have in your hand.

Work out the slack and adjust the position of the strands to form a pleasing spiral effect. This will probably take several attempts but stick with it because the end result is worthwhile.

# The Star Knot

The Star Knot was always considered by sailors to be the most difficult, and if you had that on your knot board (a sailor's CV), you were assured of a better position on board ship.

The Star Knot is an interlocking, multi-layered knot and must start from a crown (*see pages 28 and 61*) and can be tied with anything from four strands upwards. Here we show a 6-strand Star Knot.

Strands leaving a crown worked in an anti-clockwise direction is my favourite way of starting. The crown should be as tight as possible. Form a bight in the green strand with the working end underneath. Form the same bight in the white and pass the white working end through the green bight.

Continue with blue, black, red and yellow. At this point, put the green working end through the yellow bight to complete this level.

Remove the slack but only gently. At this stage the knot should hold itself, and you can make another crown going back on itself on top of this layer. That is, the yellow strand must go on top of the previous yellow bight. Take the yellow working end and follow the red strand, going under itself, and pass through the black bight of the first layer where the red strand comes out.

The red strand can now follow the black strand, passing through the blue bight; the blue can follow the white in the same fashion, going through the green, etc. etc.

Turn your work over, and for clarity we continue with the yellow strand, which will go through just behind where it left the original tightly-made crown, as shown by the solid arrow. Continue this with all strands.

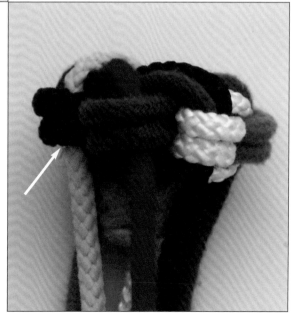

In order to complete your Star Knot, a further crown should be made to fill the centre and make the knot firmer all round.

Remove all the slack and make sure this crown is tight and secure. At this point you must decide whether you are going to continue in the same direction with some form of senate, or whether you are going to terminate at this point.

To terminate, pass each strand back down through the Star Knot.

After removing all slack, the surplus should be cut off without damaging adjoining strands.

In this example, I started with a 4-strand French senate, followed by an 8-strand Matthew Walker. Then continued with a 4-strand Doubled French senate using four lots of two-strands rather than singly. Take care when making this particular senate, that the paired strands come through together, and don't twist over or under each other. A Star Knot has been added and then a crown senate, again using strands doubled instead of singly. (*See page 125*).

Below the Star Knot, without hiding the strands back and cutting off, I have made a footrope knot, un-laid the remaining rope and brushed it out with a dog's brush. The short metal bristle kind is the best I've found. To get a nice straight tassel, dip it in a cup of very hot water for a few minutes, and brush it out again while still wet. Hang up and allow to dry.

# Making a Keyring

First let's tie a small keyring using 3mm-diameter cord. Take three pieces of cord approximately 3'3" [1m] long and find the centre, i.e. half way along its length. 1¼" [35mm] left of centre, place a temporary whipping – a constrictor knot is ideal – using thin whipping twine. Now you can either hand-twist a rope (*see page 110*) or form a 3-strand English senate (a plait commonly used for hair). Continue twisting or plaiting until a total of 2" [50mm] has been worked, keeping it as tight as possible. Fold in half, add your split ring, then ¾" [20mm] below the top of the loop now formed, add a further whipping constrictor knot.

Remove the first whipping from the three strands. You now have six strands. Keeping the two centre strands out of the way – tying them loosely in a simple knot and hanging it from an overhead hook will solve this nicely – take the four remaining strands and form a footrope knot (*see page 67*). Remove as much slack as possible until the doubled footrope knot is hard and tight.

Now, using all six strands, start your crowning (*see pages 28 and 61*). Having no core, this is called a crown senate. After eight crowns, form a Star Knot (*see page 120*).

After the Star Knot, fill in with two more crowns and bring the strands up through your finished work so that they are as shown below.

When all is tight, cut off the surplus strands as tight to the work as possible, without damaging adjacent cords.

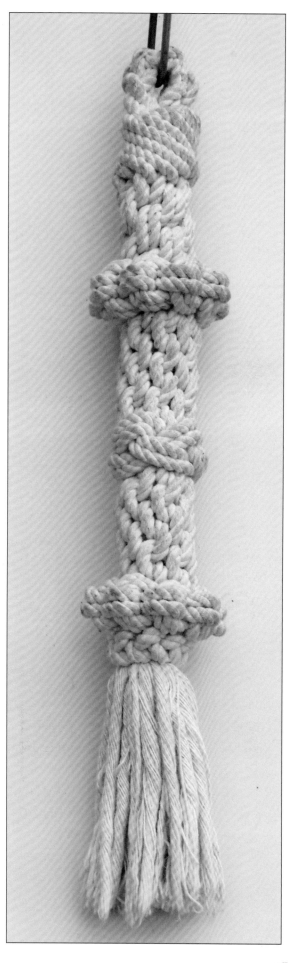

# Tiller Tassels

By this stage, you are no doubt ready to create your own designs. My favourite tiller tassel is somewhat grubby now, as it accompanies me on my talks and gets thrown in and out of my sea-chest with obvious results.

Depending on the length and thickness of the tiller tassel you need, choose thicker cord for this. Four strands of 4mm cotton rope makes an attractive, chunky tiller tassel.

You can of course make it in exactly the same style as the keyring, or you can make it longer and fatter using eight strands. The choice is yours, and you can use any configuration of the knots and senates you have learned here.

Some people find it is easier to hang their work from a hook, once the top loop has been formed.

# Ben's Bights 'n Pieces

Top left: *Barge fender on Tunnel Tug No. 4,* Gloucester *at Saul Festival 2008.* Top right: Gloucester's *Dwarf's trousers.* Below: *Barge fender on* MSC Frodsham. *Note the sacrificial Turk's heads – 16 of them.*

*From the largest to the smallest . . .* Top: *Offering up the 22-ft rope core for a Dutch barge fender.*
Bottom right: *Then covering it!* Bottom left: *Ben works on a tingle button at Saul Festival 2008.*

Top: *A brand new button*. Centre left: *A barge fender*. Centre right: *Donuts anyone?* Bottom left: *A button, bottle fenders and dwarf's trousers in black*. Bottom right: *White bottle fenders look good but are rather impractical for daily use*.

*A matching tipcat and button for a customer.*

*A new pair of Dwarf's Trousers, ready for collection.*

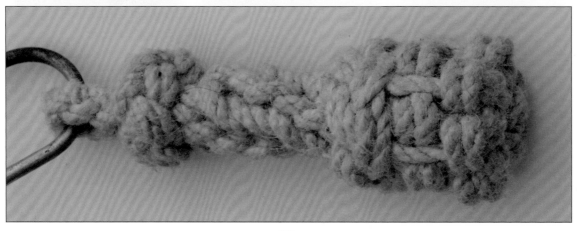

*Guess what this is? Here's a clue...*

*These random designs can be made into a keyring, a tiller tassel, a bell pull, or anything you wish. Now you can have fun making up your own.*

In late 2006, the Marine Co-ordinator for the yet-to-be-filmed *Golden Compass*, was walking along the towpath at Saul Junction, and noticed Ben's butty, *Lyra*. There was no connection, but as we all now know, the young heroine of the film is also called Lyra. The two men got chatting, and Ben was subsequently asked to dress Ma Costa's barge, the vessel hired by the film-makers for the film. Ben spent several months preparing fenders, swan necks, tingle buttons, Turk's heads and sundry fancy ropework.

As filming was about to begin, the film company discovered that the owner of the Dutch barge was not qualified to skipper the vessel. In consternation they turned to Ben to ask if he knew anyone who could do it. Ben was able to produce the appropriate certificate and he was duly offered the rôle.

There followed many, many weeks of filming, in the Wash and on the River Thames, with a full cast, helicopters aloft, camera, lights, orchestra! Sad to relate, however, virtually the whole lot ended up on the cutting room floor. If you go to see *The Golden Compass*, don't blink or you'll miss the few seconds the barge is visible.

Above: *Ben dressed for his rôle as skipper on Ma Costa's barge in* The Golden Compass, *destined for the cutting room floor.*
Right: *The swan neck, tingle button and some of the Turk's heads Ben made for Ma Costa's barge.*
Photos: C. Ruth

Above: *Now that's what you call a Turk's Head*. Right inset: *Mounted on a low-loader, ready for the off.*
Below: *Ben supervises the positioning of his fenders on Ma Costa's barge at Shepperton Studios. Photos: C. Ruth*
*See more photos from* The Golden Compass *on the film's official website: www.goldencompassmovie.com*

*Sailing down the River Thames.*

*Lots of dry ice was called for, in nearby rowing boats. Inside, Ma Costa's barge was filled with massive amounts of lighting equipment and there were cables everywhere.*

*Filming took place on the Thames and in the Wash, off Kings Lynn. Such a shame no-one saw any of the footage.*

*These photographs are from the BBC website, see right.*

http://news.bbc.co.uk/cbbcnews/hi/newsid_6050000/newsid_6053100/6053166.stm#

Above: *Lyra and Knot Krazy, huddled in the early morning mist at Saul Junction.*
Photo: C. Ballinger
Inset: *The boatman's cabin on Lyra, c. 1935.*
Right: *Lyra's swan neck in misty sunshine. And cobwebs.* Photo: P. Ballinger

I hope you have started at the front of this book
and worked your way through from the simpler knots
to the more complex.

This book was never intended to be an encyclopaedia of knots
and there are hundreds more out there for you to research,
learn and hopefully, enjoy. There are many, many excellent knot books
available, that concentrate on specific items or individual knots.
You name it and you'll no doubt find it.

Please feel free to contact the
International Guild of Knot Tyers
who will be happy to share information
and offer plenty of encouragement.
http://www.igkt.net/index.php